MW00572264

Praise f

"A multivalent approach to ~~destroying nasty magic sent your way.~~ With techniques from tarot to smoke cleansing, from unhexing your hearth to handling hired spirits, help yourself with this handy guide to counter curses."

—Amy Blackthorn, author of *Blackthorn's Botanical Magic*

"*Hex Twisting* is the book you want but didn't know you needed. Not only does Diana break down questions to ask along the way, but she also encourages readers to look more closely at their lives and learn to trust what they know before they step into action. After all, no curse is unbreakable, she reminds us."

—Irisanya Moon, author of *Reclaiming Witchcraft*

"Powerful, informative, and witty, this book addresses complex subjects with clarity and practical, experience-based wisdom to offer workable solutions to combat the turmoil of hexes, curses, troublesome spirits and so much more. Diana Rajchel has gifted the witchcraft community with an invaluable guide that should be a must-read for all magical practitioners."

—Michael Furie, author of *Spellcasting for Beginners*

"The author's warm (and often a little wicked) sense of humor is balanced by compassionate and heartfelt moments dealing with the aftermath of spiritual intrusion and lingering magical trauma … *Hex Twisting* shows just how clearly dealing with curses and counter-curses is and has always been a part of magical practice, and it invites the reader to build upon that history in ways that align with their own ethical codes. It's a smart, funny, and engaging read."

—Cory Thomas Hutcheson, author of *New World Witchery* and host of the *New World Witchery* podcast

HEX
TWISTING

© Nathan McCann

About the Author

Diana Rajchel is a spirit worker, diviner, and metaphysical problem-solver. She has worked with magick and pushed at its edges for more than twenty-five years. She runs a metaphysical problem-solving service with her life partner Synty and her business partner Nikki—and often enough, it gets pretty weird.

HEX
TWISTING

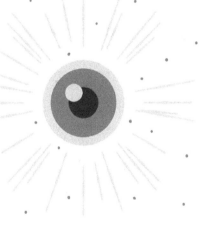

Counter-Magick Spells for the Irritated Witch

DIANA RAJCHEL

Llewellyn Publications
Woodbury, Minnesota

FIRST EDITION
Third Printing, 2022

Book design by Samantha Peterson
Cover design by Kevin R. Brown
Editing by Laura Kurtz
Interior art by Llewellyn Art Department

Llewellyn Publications is a registered trademark of Llewellyn Worldwide Ltd.

Library of Congress Cataloging-in-Publication Data
Names: Rajchel, Diana, author.
Title: Hex twisting : countermagick spells for the irritated witch / Diana Rajchel.
Description: First edition | Woodbury, Minnesota : Llewellyn Publications, 2021. | Includes bibliographical references and index. | Summary: "A more advanced book on countering hexes, curses, and magickal malfeasance"-- Provided by publisher.
Identifiers: LCCN 2021039609 (print) | LCCN 2021039610 (ebook) | ISBN 9780738765389 (paperback) | ISBN 9780738765969 (ebook)
Subjects: LCSH: Magic.
Classification: LCC BF1621 .R35 2021 (print) | LCC BF1621 (ebook) | DDC 133.4/3--dc23/eng/20211007
LC record available at https://lccn.loc.gov/2021039609
LC ebook record available at https://lccn.loc.gov/2021039610

Llewellyn Publications
A Division of Llewellyn Worldwide Ltd.
2143 Wooddale Drive
Woodbury, MN 55125-2989
www.llewellyn.com

Printed in the United States of America

To those beings who steadfastly refuse
to believe in the "impossible."

CONTENTS

ACKNOWLEDGMENTS

The following people and more were instrumental in making this and my previous work come to be. The depths of my gratitude hit the magma layers of the earth.

Thanks to:

Dawn Frederick of Red Sofa Literary Agency for her fierce protection; Elysia Gallo for her long-suffering patience and keen eye for detail; Kat Neff for making sure my particular madness gets seen; Synty Boehm, Tom Leidy, Nikki Jobin, and Omni Rogers-Mueller for saving my life while providing amoral support; Jennifer Martinez for the frequent guinea-pig opportunities, egg rolls, and wine; Ivo Dominguez Jr., Robert Deans, Sean Black, Lea Arellano, and Christine Rossi for the mentorship and wisdom; Lance Reynolds for the moral support and nonjudgment at my more dubious decisions and experiments; Kit Johnson-Glassel for helping me find my way to freedom; Azazel and Belial for so many reasons; Grandma E for the pearls, the wisdom, and the beating heart; and to my dad—he *did* tell me I'd have days like the ones that led to the creation of this book ... the bastard just forgot to say I'd have so many.

A special thank you goes to the late and well-respected Geoffrey Bayley. His discussion with me about karma from the perspective of a person raised in Hinduism was invaluable and made *Hex Twisting* a better book. Geoffrey, you took time to discuss something deep with a stranger; I am grateful it gave me a chance to meet you before you left.

ONE

WHAT IS COUNTERMAGICK AND WHY IS IT NECESSARY?

Despite dogma intended to reassure the public of witchcraft's safety, it has always been true that "less friendly practitioners," in author of *Mastering Witchcraft*'s Paul Huson's words, exist. In non-European cultures, this cursing is considered a fact of life; in certain shamanic traditions, people learn their skills by engaging in metaphysical battles with one another. These conflicts reveal one essential truth: magick workers are human, and like all humans, magickal people have egos. When their egos decide to run amok, they have tools to make a situation much worse than mundane human conflict.

What Is Countermagick?

Countermagick is what you do after someone leaves you the metaphysical equivalent of a flaming bag of dog poop at your front door. In this situation, you clean up the mess and then take steps to prevent it from happening again.

As happens in flaming dog poop situations, you usually have some idea who left it. Sometimes you don't. Whoever did it, you likely want to hold those people accountable.

When someone resolves conflicts via magick, the tools of protection also serve as the tools of warfare. In Wicca, ritual tools remind practitioners of magick's duality and life itself: an athame (ritual blade) is a double-edged blade that reminds the user that what can heal can harm. For witches of other crafts, we understand that actions have consequences—and sometimes we must become those consequences.

While perhaps a few people in the world really can get by on love and light alone, even the kindest folks will sooner or later encounter someone determined to start some trouble. All too often, the person targeted may let it slide if it happens just to them. However, even the most white-light workers will call up their shadows when someone starts in on friends and family. A lot of witches have a wicked style of love; when called to protect friends and family, we will fight dirty, even if it means every horse head in the metaphorical stable winds up in someone's bed.

Many spells function as offensive protection. In contrast to defensive protections, these castings *counter* negative energy, and in many cases are far more effective than simple defense. Consider the difference between defensive and offensive warding spells for a house. House wards that passively resist intrusion and act as inanimate shields dissipate under continued pressure.

However, someone can make active house wards that turn into the spiritual equivalent of rabid bats. Angry sky rodents stop shenanigans far more effectively than wards that only block energy.

What Is Negative Magick?

Negative magick is any occult energy structure intended to harm on a physical, emotional, or spiritual level. While often cast for petty reasons, negative work itself is not inherently evil. As explained above, sometimes the best way to protect you and yours is to destroy what sets out to take it.

As in all magick that involves sending and transforming energy, if you have the will and emotion behind your intention, you need not use a formal spell. Even so, there exists a set of offensive spells common to magickal lexicon. Until now, they had a mostly unspoken scale as to how much harm each can do. From mildest to most severe, the four most common negative workings are:

- Jinxes
- Hexes
- Crosses
- Curses

Jinxes

Jinxes cause minor inconveniences rather than outright harm. That tradition where you say something simultaneously with the other person, and someone yells "jinx!" is a small, fun-loving example of this kind of spell. By yelling "jinx!" you wish the other person minor bad luck until they "pay" you. Traditionally, you break the jinx in this case by buying the sender a cola. More common jinxes are used when someone feels mildly disrespected.

These spells usually involve trivial misfortune, the type where you question if it's worth the bother because the inconveniences caused by the jinx are so small and fade so fast.

Hexes

Hexes involve targeted bad luck. Depending on how angry the caster is, some can cause serious pain. Old-school hexes aim to wound the target's ego as much as the body. Popularized spells might be things like making your ex-boyfriend's hair fall out or causing someone to have an expensive emergency at a financially delicate time. While Medieval hexes such as boils and sores have mostly gone by the wayside thanks to medical advancement, some workers have modernized their methods, adapting to current conditions like triggering allergic reactions for their hexes.

Crosses

A cross blocks your path. Those who have never experienced them might think a crossing sounds minor. It's anything but. No accomplishment can happen when someone has magickally crossed you. If you have any goal at all, just having an intention while under such a spell will halt any progress. It's difficult to give a concrete example of a crossing because it's so all-encompassing—you functionally can't do anything. Any progress already made becomes rot instead. People cast crosses to keep you in the same place emotionally, geographically, and financially.

Curses

Curses are spells cast to cause permanent damage to body, mind, and spirit. Some hold the intention of killing, or, worse, causing soul-death. While some work fast, well-constructed curses have a slow burn as they consume the victim's morale and life. Because of complex issues related to generational trauma, genetics, and economics, curses can sometimes exploit extant genetic illnesses such as addiction.

Why Attempt Harm with Magick?

Wouldn't punching someone be faster? Why not just try to get along?

All people have good and bad in them, and most people have some vulnerability that can bring out their worst selves.

To understand negative magick to counter it, you need to understand this: all hexing and cursing came about as survival magick. Hoodoo, especially famed for some of its vicious curses, got labeled as "black" magick, supposedly for its crueler aspects. The reputation came about because people of African and indigenous origin practiced it. The magick practiced in the United States happened as a direct result of slavery and people doing what they had to do to survive tortures that put the *Malleus Malleficarum* to shame. Before mostly white Europeans figured out that Black people practiced magick, negative magick was just magick, no color-coding necessary. Hexing (or sometimes domination) either gave you power in a desperate situation or demonstrated the strength of will to those that might otherwise attempt such an influence. In the industrial world, we still need hexes and curses. We also have room to *not* need this magick, depending on the level of the privilege conferred at birth. For people who live in situations where the tools of justice do not serve them, the ability to hex is a gift and multigenerational tool meant to relieve injustice.

The Dead Dogma about Hexes

As a child of mid-1990s witchcraft, I too sucked down Satanic Panic era works, either warning of the "evils" of Satanism or insisting that *all* witches Don't Do Those Things, no cursing, no baby eating—your goats and pets are safe. At least speaking from my own experience, the latter has for the most part proven true outside of specific cultural witchcraft practices that involve animal sacrifice in a profound and sacred way.

My experience began to belie the *no cursing* claim only a few years into my practice. I committed myself to the practice of witchcraft in 1996 and had to deal with my first psychic attack by 1998. It was aggressive, malicious, and had I not sought shamanic help, I might still suffer. I was not the only person in my acquaintance group attacked. No resolution to these attacks could happen for anyone in my community until we talked about what was happening. To have that conversation, we had to break with the dogma that witches don't curse.

From that time on, my realities stopped matching the books I consumed and the common wisdom advocated by other witches at the time. When I initially reached out for help, my community derided me and turned away—so I had to seek help from more experienced people outside of my culture. What those people taught me even as I evolved my practice has saved not just my life but my soul.

As you develop a spiritual practice, the magickal world becomes an extension of the wild kingdom. No matter how much making nice you attempt, there is always some other magick worker out there thinking they're a lion and marking their territory (usually metaphorically) to declare dominance. One might mistake you for a gazelle. It then falls to you to demonstrate that you are not prey, and you are not playing. That often demands setting aside the 1990s "harm none" standards if you want at the very least a good night's sleep.

What about Karma and the Law of Three?

Karma is not math or physics. It's not even a measure of sin. As used in Wicca, karma began as cultural misappropriation and has expanded to a different, somewhat inaccurate definition of what it is and how it works. In Buddhism and Hinduism, karma refers to a debt that you incur in the process of fulfilling your dharma during this lifetime. *Dharma* refers to a moral balance that accounts for the entire universe and the individual. How you fare in your lifetime remains unknown until you die.

When Western witches use the term "karma," they mean "consequences." When you treat people terribly, eventually people treat you the same. On occasion, ancestors, deities, and other spirits intervene, but no one guarantees or regulates when that happens. There are complete jerks that get hit by buses, have pianos fall on them, and get bird poop in their cleavage every day. Some genuinely decent people have the same things happen to them just as often. There is no clear determination of whether the universe is cruel or random or whether some people's ancestors are perhaps a bit less than discerning when it comes to protecting their descendants. We use magick to help consequences along, yes, but it's a big universe with many moving parts. We can only control so much and cope so long knowing that a significant portion of what we think we control is an illusion.

When someone casts a hex or counterwork, you need to prepare for consequences, not because some invisible space nanny wants you to make nice. Magick kind-of-sort-of follows the laws of thermodynamics. Some bad vibes sent out come back to people because that's just the way that energy works. Making an effort to introduce more kindness can help this situation, but again: the universe is full of moving parts, humans are full of traumas, and there's no telling what the person in your life with the bad personality will do next.

So long as jealousy and entitlement exist in the world, so will curses. Covetousness and rage are the fundamental emotional pulses upon which spiteful, rather than protective, hexing operates. Since we are all interconnected, we can sometimes focus on certain connections over others and send energy to those affiliations, good or bad, an expression of our personal wills. Sometimes we can even force someone who would ordinarily refuse our negativity to accept it. Our entanglements are complex, and so sometimes the seemingly simple rules of "just don't tick anyone off" can't apply. No matter how kind you are and how cleanly you live, someone may try to send you some unhappiness. This book covers what to do about it when someone does.

TWO

AM I CURSED?
Methods of Curse Diagnostics

For the last fifty years, the party line for Neopagans responding to this question has been "probably not!" My experience, however, conflicts with this. Just as dismissing someone with a health complaint instead of checking on it can lead to complications, dismissing someone with a curse concern can make their situation worse. It's always better to attempt to verify a curse than to dismiss it out of hand.

A culture of silent embarrassment surrounds those who do experience targeted negative magick, not just because of that outdated attitude that they don't exist, but because of an implication that you must be an especially bad person if someone cursed you. In this way, it's no different from blaming the victims of any other assault.

When someone books me for a consultation to ask if they are cursed, I say, "Let's make an effort to rule that out." About half the time, my clients do have some degree of cursing happening to them not because cursing is common but because I draw people that need the type of help I can provide. That said, cursing is becoming increasingly common, which makes the procedure of dismissing the possibility without first looking deeper spiritually irresponsible. I do not think the amount of curse cases I encounter is typical of most practitioners. My numbers on this are anecdotal, my clients confidential, and my own experience notoriously strange. I can't offer empirical data on this, nor should I. Other practitioners whom I greatly respect say they rule out more curses than they confirm. I believe them.

When a reading indicates that yes, there's a curse, the question changes. It shifts from "Am I cursed?" to "How severely and in what way?" While most people want to know why someone sent them concentrated negativity, knowing why rarely resolves the problem.

In the process of curse verification, I perform a series of due diligence checks. Besides asking about mental and physical health and daily stressors that might replicate curse symptoms, I also try to get a sense of the person in front of me. I do my best to account for jobs and activities that society frowns on or family dynamics that encourage shame and failure feelings. Most cursed individuals are kind, accomplished people who sense the bad energy after receiving the brunt of someone's jealousy. Every so often, however, I meet a cursed person with a rotten personality. While I question the effort (their toxicity curses them enough) some people earn enough contempt that there's almost no question as to why someone cursed them. I try to refer especially nasty and uncooperative individuals to a therapist; unfortunately, the people who might benefit most from therapy are usually the most likely to refuse it.

Am I Cursed? 11

The curses I see are often small, and I can generally help my client resolve those permanently in one session. Small scale antagonism such as jinxes and hexes happen more often and come off easily. Curses and crosses take effort, planning, energy, DNA theft, and expertise to manifest. Lesser mean-spirited workings only require small doses of spite to happen spontaneously. That toxicity need not come from a magickal practitioner. The barest whisper of wanting misfortune to visit another from someone with a spiritual practice can fire off a work of malice.

Accidental whammies clean off easily in most situations. It's the deliberate stuff that demands inspection. As a best practice, clear the random yuckiness as much as possible before you consult a psychic or do your divination to determine if anything was intentional. Chapter three outlines some simple, standard methods of self-cleansing you can use to remove petty nastiness. It may turn out that you just needed a proper washing and you won't need more!

Symptoms of Curses and Other Negative Works

For the sake of brevity, from this point forward, I refer to magick sent with full negative intent as curses. Whatever the size and impact of the working, people experience curses either externally or internally. The more complicated curses work on both levels.

When people experience curses externally, they often experience them initially as an inexplicable run of bad luck. Yes, in some circumstances those misfortunes happen because of spirit attempting to teach us something. Sometimes the stars have selected you for a slapstick routine. But when that unlucky streak runs past a week to ten days, it's time to rule out cosmic mischief and start seeking out other causes. For minor stuff—and always start with the small stuff and work upward—smoke cleansing and an Epsom salt bath removes most unclean/ill-intended energies. The vast majority of people can use just one of these low-grade cleansings, and all the weirdness stops immediately. People who use these cleansings successfully often report to me a feeling of lifting afterward. However, if you still feel off after performing said ablutions, start looking for patterns within the bad luck.

Think hard about where and when bad luck happens. Does it persist in a specific area of your life? For example, if you want to start a business and suddenly everything related to your business meets an obstacle, look at your competitors and anyone objecting to your endeavor. Let's say you boot up your computer only to find that multiple pieces of software you use suddenly stopped working for no obvious reason. Then when you try to print something out, your printer driver fails, and you must reinstall. Because of this, you miss a deadline to file some critical licensing papers. To top it off, your business partner ends up in a minor car accident while attempting to talk to a potential landlord about a site for your business, and now money earmarked for renting a retail space must divert to car repair.

If one or two of these things happened, it might just be Mercury retrograde or an especially bad day, the result of sleep deprivation. When so many things happen at once, all of them related to you and a known goal you have, then it's time to rule out something less benign than everyday life chaos. Why someone cursed you isn't important. However, it is important to acknowledge that when you attempt to succeed in your life, it does give some people a motive for shenanigans. In starting a business, someone among your family or friends might be jealous and feel their self-worth drop upon witnessing your progress. You might unknowingly be in competition with another business for retail space. The people running that business might have some activated spell or prayer energy that ensures they get that exact spot and will keep any potential renters away from it. In an extreme version of this situation, a land spirit may just not want you conducting your business on it. A little thought about who might have an issue with you can often reveal the reason for a possible curse, if not necessarily their identity or their means.

At other times, the purpose of the attacks remains opaque. You suddenly encounter a string of aggressive parking spot thieves, followed by birds pooping on you as you walk to work before important meetings. People you see daily suddenly express hostility despite no inciting incidents. There isn't a clear pattern, but you know someone wants you to know they disapprove of you. As long as the incidents remain annoying but not dangerous, the who, why, and how may not matter, so long as you can break the jinx on you before the added daily stress takes an emotional toll.

The worst external curses resemble hauntings. In the most serious cases, someone employs a spirit to harass the target, so the curse is functionally a haunting. These spirits may create an oppressive atmosphere in someone's home, move objects, or cause electrical disturbances. If burning cedar incense with the windows open does not clear the negative energy, reevaluate the situation: it's likely you are either dealing with a different type of spirit than the type someone contracts for a short-term haunting or someone is taking a conscious and active role in sending you negativity, realized you got rid of the spirit, and sent it back.

Possibly the most insidious, effective, and dangerous curses function by using a tiny piece of internal energy, triggering the victim to act on themselves. This style of malediction takes skill and considerable self-knowledge on the part of the sufferer to identify. These knockbacks can manifest as physical or cognitive symptoms. When experiencing physical symptoms, it's natural and wise to assume they are medical. A medical explanation does not rule out a curse, but it makes the possibility of one far less likely. Even if the physical problem stems from a curse, proper treatment at least partially addresses and resolves it, making it worth the effort of seeing a doctor.

When thinking about internal cursing and illness, it's helpful to consider the ancient world perspective on demons. People of this time viewed demons as parasitic entities in the bloodstream. We no longer consider parasites part of the invisible world, but there are parallels between physical and magickal "infection." Both must fight our natural immune systems. Indicators of internal cursing can include but are not limited to dizzy spells, disorientation, insomnia, lingering colds, inexplicable depression, and excess sleeping. If these symptoms continue after you receive medical treatment, investigate metaphysical avenues in addition to following your doctor's advice. Bear in mind that mood swings, undesired altered perception such as hallucinations, and bouts of paranoia converge as both symptoms of mental illness and cursing symptoms because of the long-held stigma applied to people with neurological imbalances. A particularly crafty attacker will want to discredit you to keep the punishment going, and you may need to be patient as you seek someone willing to help you.

While difficult when sick or exhausted, try to pay attention to your inner chatter without letting it engulf your attention. Your inner world can offer clues when there's more to your illness than you thought. If you have recurring dreams about specific people, especially ones you dislike or barely know, it may signal trouble connected to them. It may also signal someone playing to your prejudices as a mislead. Pay attention to nagging feelings. Write down the stream of consciousness flowing through your mind when you first wake up, during an emotional crisis, or right before bed. Doing so may help you identify either the source of your disruption or pinpoint triggers you have that exacerbate any difficult-to-cope-with emotions.

A complication to keep in mind: sometimes someone does receive hordes of negative energy not because of any intention but because their intuitive abilities expanded. Empaths especially run into this, though the problem is far from exclusive to them. The collective human ability to perceive energy extends beyond the concepts of good or bad. Increased power often translates first to enhanced awareness, and becoming more aware of what else shares the world with you has, at times, unpleasant side effects.

For those who flipped through this chapter first because you are worried, the following gives you references to verify or dismiss a curse. If you see any symptoms you are experiencing on the list, you *might* be cursed. Do all you can to account for your global context before coming to that conclusion. For example, say you experience strange temperature variations throughout the day. Does it follow you outside of your home? Does your home have drafts? Did your chills stop when you put on a sweater? Have you tested negative for any illness, are not approaching perimenopause, have just invested in excellent home insulation, and are positive you don't have food poisoning? If the latter happens, take account of your daily activities. You might, for instance, walk past a cemetery on the way to class every day and drop your finished cup of coffee over the fence. If you do that often enough, something that stays in the cemetery may take notice and follow you around until you show some respect.

If you find that you recognize yourself in three or more symptom areas, skip to the section on diagnostics, using divination tools to verify whether it's a curse or something else is going on.

External Curse Symptoms

- Runs of bad luck, exceeding five to seven adverse incidents within one week. They can include items breaking, messages failing to deliver, and missing opportunities or fun events by only moments. It often involves at least one catastrophic personal event.

- Unusual, persistent, and frequent hostility from strangers.

- Quarreling at home and with coworkers when outside the norm

- A general feeling of oppression in your home, especially in places you sleep or relax.

- Strings of failures connected to specific endeavors when other projects remain unaffected.

- Poltergeist-like activities in your home, vehicle, or workplace. Cabinet doors opening suddenly and violently, items falling off shelves, and loud noises such as banging or hitting.

Internal Curse Symptoms

- Catching illnesses more often than usual, even when it is not cold or flu season; flare-ups in existent chronic illnesses that are out of sync with their typical patterns.

- Abnormal bodily sensations: chills or heat, pressure, sense of electric currents usually concentrated in the heart, spleen, solar plexus, throat, and sacral chakras; feeling invisible bodies attaching to places on the aura.

- Dizziness, inability to concentrate, difficulty grounding and centering, and such exercises failing to help you reorient.

- Exacerbation of addictions and addictive coping behaviors. This is not limited to only substance abuse but also applies to toxic relationship patterns, such as contacting an abusive ex partner or friend.

- Unusually low impulse control that can't be explained by medication, such as eating and drinking things that you know will cause distress.

- Sleep disruptions, nightmares, or excess sleep.

"I Might Be Cursed!" Protocol

1. Try to ground and center as best you can. Repeat grounding exercises multiple times per day. You can find exercises for these skills on the internet.

2. Take a bath or shower. You may want to mix yourself an herb bath using the ingredients list in chapter three.

3. Perform an egg or fire cleansing. Instructions for this are in chapter four.

4. Reiki can help in many but not all circumstances—see a practitioner and heal what you can. Assess the day after your session what, if any, negativity remains.

Six Methods for Diagnosing a Curse

The most effective curse diagnostics work from a place of disconfirmation—first, try to rule it *out*. Most of what follows assumes you have already expended rigorous energy looking for the logical explanations, and with those entirely or mostly ruled out, you need to consider the spiritual possibilities. What follows are methods for curse *verification*. Use these methods when you know you have some metaphysical issue but are not sure whether it is a curse or something else.

Find a trusted, skeptical, yet mystic-friendly companion to help you run the following divination checks. You may wish to seek a professional reader versed in cursing and energy clearing; people with this knowledge are more common than they were near the turn of the twenty-first century. Search in Facebook groups and look into which members of certain groups are recommended (and who to avoid). Working with communities that appear more fact-based than intuition-driven in their discussions go a long way in finding reputable professional help.

As much as you can, it's important to muster a genuinely open mind about whatever is happening to you or any person you care about who might carry a curse. Affecting a hopeful attitude of "that's probably not it, but just in case" helps maintain morale when investigating possibilities. After all, if you start from a paranoia-driven rabbit hole, you may damage some important relationships in your life—thus cursing yourself!

If you go to a reader to explore the possibility of a curse, initially avoid asking about any magical malfeasance unless you already know and trust the reader. Open the conversation with "I seem to be confronting a lot of blocks/running into more turmoil than normal. I am hoping that divination can help me understand the cause and perhaps get a few ideas as to what to do about it." A skilled reader will focus on your emotional context and underlying causes. If you sense that bringing up cursing can help bring clarity to the reading, do so. If an ethical practitioner sees a curse, they may or may not bring it up in a first session, but *any* practitioner will strongly suggest a program of spiritual cleansing upon seeing a negative energy attachment. When performing these diagnostics, keep in mind that with the exception of the pendulum and egg reading, even if a negative spell is identified on your person, most methods do not indicate how much damage the curse has done. For example, you might pull the Tower card—yes, someone did curse you—but that doesn't tell you whether someone has lined up a piano to fall on you as you walk down the street or whether you spilling coffee on your laptop fulfilled the conditions of the spell.

If you want to assess the severity of a negative energy "hit" after confirming a curse as you work with these methods, I recommend using dice with six sides or more. Lower numbers indicate lesser impact; higher rolls indicate greater. Anything that falls below a 3 (on a 3 to 12 scale) should indicate incidental or weak energy. In most cases, when the "hit" level is that low, all someone needs is a bath or similar cleansing. While I don't use this method every time I encounter someone who tests positive for cursing, in cases where someone comes back for help more than once, this does let me spend a little less time guessing how long it might take to reset their energy to healthy.

Method 1: Pendulum Diagnosis

A pendulum serves as a quick and dirty "yes or no" tool. First, cleanse and calibrate your pendulum. To cleanse, fumigate it with frankincense or spray it with Florida Water. To calibrate it, ask your pendulum to show you how it says yes, then no. Always ask your tool if it wants to work with you. Obtaining consent goes a long way toward accuracy in this type of spiritual work. Next, fine-tune your pendulum by asking a few yes-or-no questions you already know the answer to. Questions might include "Is my name ___?" Or "Does one plus one equal two?"

The simplest way to check for negativity is for a partner—not the suspected curse holder—to hold the pendulum and ask, "Is X cursed?" Estimate the force of the swing on the answer, especially if it says yes. A strong swing suggests the pendulum senses a great deal of energy around the question you just asked. If the intention behind the energy is to cause only minor inconvenience or has less effort or intention in it, the pendulum may respond with less force. The pendulum may barely move at all if the querent walked through the metaphysical equivalent of a mud puddle on the way home. In that case, the energy was incidental, not personal, and will take just a little bit of cleaning to stop the problem.

If the pendulum answers yes to the curse question, next ask it "Where?" To get that answer, stand behind the querent and hold the tool to each of the major chakra points. Depending on its communication style, the pendulum will either swing to a yes or a no over a chakra. In some cases, it may jerk in a particular direction. After you check the seven major chakras, check the head's crown and the four spiritual chakras connected to the center of the crown chakra. The clogged or damaged chakra will likely indicate the nature of the curse. On the crown points, the center of the crown indicates sovereignty. One crown point is sense of self, one is past lives, one is ancestors, and the final point affects your ability to hear guidance from spirits. In some cases, finding this spot can even show how malicious energy entered the body, making it easier to cleanse and remove.

Method 2: Coin Toss Diagnosis

Some people do not trust pendulum readings because personal biases can and do affect them. Thus, if you already believe you are cursed, the pendulum may indicate such even if incorrect, no matter how well calibrated it is. If this seems likely, just toss a coin instead. If your coins have prosperity working on them, or if you're concerned that picking up a cursed coin has contributed to your experiences, then borrow a coin from someone you don't know.

Name heads for no curse and tails for a curse, and flip. Thank the coin and any person you borrowed it from when you return it.

Method 3: Tarot Diagnosis

Tarot can diagnose a curse without input from other tools, but I prefer it after checking with another method, such as the pendulum. I then use the cards to glean the specific spell. Determining those results comes later. For this chapter, I only go over whether the tarot verifies a curse.

I rarely use formal tarot spreads. Instead, I let the cards talk; they tell me what order to lay them in and sometimes why and we go from there. Since people who gave me feedback on these diagnostics told me that they need card and meaning with placements, I designed this layout for curse diagnostics to help people with more linear minds than my own. Full disclosure: I have only used this layout in tests to prepare for this book. The cards mentioned are the most likely candidates of "yup, there's a curse." Even so, there are no absolutes, especially not in tarot. When there is magickal malice afoot, the cards tend to point to it with major arcana. Minor arcana around that major tend to spell out who did it and what they did—the details of which are included in a later chapter.

TAROT LAYOUT: IS THIS A CURSE OR SOMETHING ELSE?

It's a little strange to use facedown cards in tarot, but in recent times I've found it's an effective way of "grabbing" energies that prefer to remain hidden. While it can reveal negative workings others took pains to cover, the facedown/faceup method can also show my client pieces of themselves they tend to ignore or disown. All too often, these disowned parts are experienced as curses or are used as tools in a curse against someone. When the client continues to

avoid those aspects, repressed energies often build up and a gey-
ser of negativity can appear as a curse to the receiver. Should this
happen when reading for another person, please encourage that
person to seek mental health support; it is an excellent practice for
readers to have resources available for referrals.

Reading requires thirteen cards: the center, which indicates the
querent's place, and three cards each facedown and faceup on
either side. The facedown cards indicate hidden or suppressed
aspects of the querent or the situation; the faceup cards tell us
what is known or what we can perceive with ease.

The surface card often reveals negative energy or a curse that
ran afoul of someone's shadows and traumas. The underlying
cards tend to show where that person may have repressed emotions that act like a curse; if the Moon shows up, for example, that
is where the curse is hitting them in their psyche.

There are only three cards in the entire tarot I consider "high
likelihood" indicators of a curse. Even then, unless all three appear
together, consider other possibilities. Those cards are the Devil

upright, the Tower upright or reversed, and the Moon upright or reversed.

THE DEVIL, UPRIGHT
(LIKELIHOOD: MODERATE TO HIGH)

The Devil is a high-context card that can alternately deliver a blunt warning or signal subtle pleasures about to arrive. Since this card strongly suggests sexual energy, it also changes in meaning based on the querent's lifestyle. For most people, the Devil's upright aspect refers to addiction, nonconsensual dominance, and violence. In most cases after ruling out the aforementioned situations, it indicates a person who feels genuine malice toward the querent. This card often shows up for people in abusive relationships.

Often this person may appear as deceptive, charming, and possibly an ally. Ask the querent who is new in their life—those indicated by the Devil card usually do not wait to begin their behaviors. In most cases, the source of trouble becomes obvious during the reading. But if the person is in a romantic relationship with the identified person, they may resist extricating themselves. If the resistance seems out of place, do a quiet check for mental influence (suggested by the Seven of Cups combined with the Moon or Sun reversed.) If you sense that someone violated this person's free will, a cord-cutting such as described in chapter four may break the mental influence and can help if you do not have time to perform a full banishing working.

THE TOWER, UPRIGHT AND REVERSED
(LIKELIHOOD: HIGH)

This card signals a collapse, one that is either pending or in the immediate past. Often when the Tower appears, it may take some negative energy to get the ball rolling, but someone picked something already vulnerable to destruction. Since curses and hexes are the warped opposite of love magick, it's essential to ask the querent to look at their relationship map when this appears. To do so requires making a chart of all people most immediately connected to the person, living and dead, in addition to people connected to *those connections* who may have opinions about the person at the center. Relationship maps include more than just romance and family. They include coworkers, business partners, and neighbors. Ask the querent to consider where and when a falling out happened, even if it happened to someone they know and not themselves directly. While the Tower speaks of disaster in a general sense, in the context of cursing, it mainly depicts the size of a person's feelings about the target of their ire. Unfortunately it sometimes also shows the size of the impact of the curse.

If inverted, the Tower may indicate a near-miss of cursing or something that needed to end that didn't. Additional cards can add clarity to its meaning when it appears in this aspect.

THE MOON, UPRIGHT AND REVERSED (LIKELIHOOD: HIGH)

While the Devil speaks of overt brutality, the Moon in the tarot speaks of subtle violence.

In my experience with the tarot, if this card shows up when asking about curses, there's trouble no matter the angle. After all, our emotions live within the shadows depicted, and the moon rules tides of feeling just as it does the ocean flow. Blame the patriarchy, but since the days when the Waite-Smith deck first appeared, this feminine energy card has meant hidden information, deceit, and the feeling of being overwhelmed.

It appears most often in the following curse situations:

- A false friend, someone who is nice to your face but is stabbing you in the back.

- A practitioner with the skill to cover their tracks (often this is a case where someone has employed a spirit.)

- Someone hired a spirit to do their dirty work; most spirit pacts traditionally happen by moonlight.

- You somehow caught a demon or other spirit-for-hire's attention (this is not always bad news; it depends on the demon. Remember, demons don't summon themselves).

- You failed to keep a pact with a spirit and now have a haunting to deal with until you pay the agreed price.

- In some cases, the Moon can indicate someone who lacks awareness that they cast energy when they wish someone ill. If, for instance, it's a talented child, the Fool card may appear near the Moon. The card especially appears in evil eye situations.

THE HANGED MAN INVERTED
(LIKELIHOOD: LOW TO MODERATE)

When this card appears, the situation requires further investigation. Often it indicates of the querent refusing to learn, or it can bespeak an arbitrary restriction. Linked to the story of Odin hanging from Yggdrasil to gain knowledge of the runes, when it falls direct, it tells of the necessity of suffering to learn. The card appearing in that context may translate to the querent doing something to themselves to cause their condition, which can only change after fully experiencing it. Whether the self-infliction comes from stubbornness or a spiritual influence that limits self-awareness, asking some uncomfortable questions is required, as is introspection. The Hanged Man inverted shows unnecessary suffering and self-limitation. If it refers to the querent's external circumstances, there is cursing or possibly a binding afoot. This binding may well be directly upon the person's mind or imagination rather than their circumstances.

CURSE DISCONFIRMATION CARDS

Accounting for your client's context, certain tarot cards can tell you clearly that no, there's not a curse. However, that does not mean that *nothing* is happening—whatever it is, it's just not a curse or isn't reading as one because the negative pattern is in some manner fed by the person with the problem. The following cards tend to appear often when an outside entity does not drive the strange energy. Knowledge of the likely-not-cursed cards can also help you recognize the authenticity of any professional reader that you consult, as the cards may attempt to tell you something that an unethical reader might mislead you about. These interpretations of the card do not rule out (or endorse) other ways people can use manipulation and social skills to make one another's lives difficult. They also do not rule out a person's mental state that might cause them to perceive negativity and, because of it, unconsciously breed misfortune.

THE HERMIT, UPRIGHT AND REVERSED

When the Hermit appears, it indicates that someone needs to look within to resolve their pain. There is a small exception, such as when the curse's intention is isolation. To check for that, look for the other curse cards and see where they fall. If only one or two "you are cursed" major arcana appear, it suggests a borderline situation that almost runs into someone wanting to curse the querent, who is exacerbating the situation by remaining unaware of their effect on others. Look for the Two of Swords or Five of

Cups if the intent is social ostracism; this may read as "not a curse" because the only magick involved is social engineering.

THE FOOL, DIRECT

The word "fool" in tarot might read as a harsh judgment on the querent. However, the Fool usually has a positive meaning, showing that the querent is new to a situation and may not understand everything. It also appears just as someone goes on a profound life journey. It also delivers the admonishment of "you don't know what you don't know."

THE HANGED MAN, UPRIGHT

In many ways, this is the most complicated card of the tarot because it demands that the querent sit with discomfort. Most querents who get this card would rather not deal with whatever the Hanged Man refers to and they always seem to know exactly what it's talking about. Usually the card calls for the sacrifice of old perceptions and beliefs.

ACE OF WANDS, REVERSED

The querent probably did upset someone, but little came of it. Whoever they upset might be angry but isn't motivated enough to work intentional harm. The appearance of this may also indicate a loss of motivation on the part of the client. However, if cards such as the Lovers or Three of Cups appear near the inverted Ace of wands, the offended party themselves may not have cast anything, but their friends may have. If enough people have affection for the injured party, that protective emotional energy may well find its way to you. Metaphysical things might happen without direction or intention until someone takes responsibility for the offense. It often reads more as an emotional storm rather than a curse.

Please bear in mind that no hard and fast rules declare that any appearance of a tarot card means cursed or not cursed. In divination, context matters most: as you get a sense of the querent and their life, the meaning of these cards as it pertains to them becomes clear. Sometimes the answer might be "Yes, you're cursed, someone has a doll of you that they stabbed," but other times, you may see Seven of Cups and realize that the tarot just told you that you're tired and over-emotional and that it's time to go home.

If you pulled out the tarot cards because you got a "yes" from the pendulum and nothing but "nope, that's not what's happening" cards in the reading, it might prove helpful to flip a coin (yes or no) to clarify. You may also want an unbiased friend to run a pendulum check or consult a professional reader just because personal prejudices can cloud the understanding of even the best diviners, especially when under stress.

THE FIVE OF CUPS AND THE SEVEN OF CUPS TOGETHER

When these cards appear together in a spread asking about cursing and negative energy, the message most intuited from the cards is "Go home, you're drunk." The Five of Cups depicts a figure standing in a field of spilled cups, and it often indicates emotions flowed over and a feeling of disaster. Combined with the air-like quality of the Seven of Cups and its floating, fantastical imagery in the Waite-Smith deck, the cards acknowledge this person's feelings of disaster—and that they are, at least in the moment of the reading, suffering from delusions. The people for whom these cards appear are suffering and deserve compassion—they just aren't cursed. They need a different kind of help.

That help may be a therapist. Often enough, all the person needs is a proper night's sleep, water, and a bit of protein.

Method 4: Egg Diagnostic

I use egg cleansings and readings to simultaneously lift curses and detect the source and nature of them. Some practitioners have rules about the eggs used, the color of the hen that lays them, and so on. I just use eggs bought at the grocery store or from a friend who has chickens. Black hen eggs might be superior for spiritual cleansing, but I get the success I need using whatever's on hand. While best performed with a partner, you can egg-cleanse yourself.

YOU WILL NEED:

2 eggs (one for performing, one as backup egg in case you drop the first one)

A towel in case you drop an egg

A clear, open glass container filled with water

2 broom straws (cut from any natural broom)

Roll the egg along the person's body everywhere that you both feel comfortable with. You need not touch the egg to the body for highly sensitive people: just rolling it carefully within their energetic field as far away as a foot will catch the energy of most foreign bodies. After you have finished, the egg may feel heavier. Crack the egg into the container of water and watch how the yolk falls. Cross the broom straws over top to prevent anything caught in the egg from escaping the water. Egg reading can show as much or more about someone's energetic condition as any tarot reading. While far from exhaustive, the following chart lists the most common signs and signals an egg reading can yield:

Sign	General Meaning
Bad smell/odor	If the egg has a bad smell but is fresh, this indicates illness. If it smells of sulfur, it shows a high probability of demonic energy. This conclusion must be contextual—the manifestation of demons is not always for cursing purposes. Ask the person what they've been doing metaphysically of late.
Blood in the yolk	A strong sign of malediction.
Yolk dropped to the bottom of the glass exceptionally fast	This is a symptom but not a determinant. It means someone has a lot of heavy energy on them. They may be experiencing depression or stress, or feeling burdened with life obligations.
Several pieces of white attached to the yolk	These attachments can indicate physical and spiritual attachments. Looking at the attachments' shapes can give clues as to location, effect, and intent.
Large, balloon-like bubbles in the water	Bubbles indicate situations that make someone feel trapped.
Specific faces, shapes, symbols, and patterns floating in the water	These can indicate anything from who sent energy to the nature of the person's spiritual guides. Common cursing symbols include skulls, butterflies, and swords.

Method 5: Candle Diagnostic

Of all the diagnostic methods I use, the glass jar candle is the one I like most because it shows me what's happening with great clarity. Once I dress it and light the candle, matters are literally out of my hands and I can't influence the outcome. Except when a poorly made candle finds its way to my altar, ruling wout any problems in candle production makes it possibly my most trustworthy method. Alas, it is also the least safe. Every time, I have to evaluate how firesafe my surroundings are before any candle spell.

All you need is a white glass jar candle—the size doesn't matter, so long as it's in a glass. I prefer seven-day candles, but if all you can find is an unused air freshener candle, it will work. When you choose a candle, pick one with a centered wick with wax that is neither too firm nor too soft in a glass at least ¼" thick. On the side of the glass, use a marker to write the name of the person in need of a diagnostic. Set the candle in a sink, a bathtub, or in a large bowl of water for fire safety. Light the candle and allow it to burn down completely. If the candle's glass leaves an especially dark layer of soot on the inside, burn a second candle, again with the name written on it, after the first candle burns down. If both candle jars have black soot from top to bottom, yes, you have a curse. If the candles burn clean or just leave a light layer of soot behind, you do not have a curse. If something in between happens, the person probably doesn't have a curse but may need to explore cleansing and seek spiritual assistance for a different problem.

Method 6: Higher Self

Sometimes, the easiest way to find out what's happening is to ask yourself. The higher self, sometimes referred to as the Holy Guardian Angel, contains the answers to our experiences in the material and invisible worlds. Even if new to talking to your highest self, it's worth a try. Find a place outdoors, center yourself, and ask, "Am I cursed? What's going on here?" Then trust the answer you receive.

The Risk of False Positives

Divination is an imperfect art. No matter how skilled the reader, the answers may still be wrong. Interpreting a reading relies on context and an ability to adapt to changing situations. A person may bind you one day and snip the strings on the poppet the next. Your circumstances may change to the point that cursing you has no effect because you're just not that person anymore.

My experience is most certainly not a measure of common witch experience—for me, false negatives happen more often than false positives. The people that practice hexing and cursing today do so with a great deal of study and deliberation. Often sendings come empowered with sentience. When a bad energy situation continues for more than a month after you have spent time identifying and cleansing, you may need to make several adjustments to remove it. These adjustments can include giving up a favorite vice, changing the way you talk about people, or no longer making some aspects of your life public. The following recommendations all can alleviate, if not always resolve, an ongoing attack situation.

Get a Second Opinion

While you may have the uphill battle of finding a reader that acknowledges the existence of curses and negative energy, it is not as difficult as it once was. If you need to know for sure, look to people who practice hoodoo/conjure or have a shamanic or animistic practice. They deal with curses as a regular part of reality.

Change Cleansing Methods

Just as certain parasites develop a resistance to antibiotics, metaphysical ick can also become nonresponsive to spiritual tools from overuse. Your go-to energy cleansing technique, the herbs you smoke cleanse with, and the oils you wear may all need a change from time to time. Just as you recharge and cleanse tools, freshen your methods to minimize the impact of hexes and cursing. When your methods don't cause meaningful change, hire a worker with expertise in curse removal.

Often, if a period of negativity lasts more than a month, it's likely there is more profound work to be done and you'll need someone with shamanic training who can see all the worlds involved to get the help you need. These people do high-risk work and because of that, sometimes charge high fees. You may need to put in some effort and ask around from several sources to find a trustworthy, practiced person to help you. For those of you who flipped to this chapter first, hopefully you have some clarity now. Most of you are not cursed, but you may still need clarity. With the proper tools to detect cursing, you no longer need to sit with the discomfort of wondering. Read on for how to remove curses from yourself, major and minor.

THREE

YOUR MAGICKAL BODY, YOURSELF
Cleansing, Clearing, and Spotting Influence

There is more to us than just skin and bone, and that's what lets the magick happen. Additional energy bodies feed into our immune system, nervous systems, organs, and perceptions. Each of these energetic bodies have cords threading through each chakra. The weaving together of our physical and energetic bodies gives us a link to both the world of the spiritual and the world of the material.

When we pick up too much negative energy over time, our energy bodies behave like a bloodstream overburdened with cholesterol; they become sluggish. When someone pelts us with attack energy over time, we feel it and sometimes experience it mentally, physically, and emotionally.

The Order of the Magickal Bodies

While most magickal people understand the physical body versus the aura, our magickal bodies' geographic range extends far beyond that. Certain cultures approach these bodies, their function, and their differing modes of existence in different ways that reflect what matters most in that society. For example, in Hmong culture, each person is believed to have three primary souls: one that reincarnates, one that remains on Earth, and one that travels. Some might correlate that perspective to terms used in Western psychology: the id, the ego, and the superego. Other traditions may use different names for the same energy bodies. When removing curses, it helps to understand how the person having the curse removed understands personal energy; in certain cases, their culture of origin may inform the correct steps. However, for those working from a generalized Western knowledge base, my theory is one energy map of many. Always try to work within the understanding of the person who needs help, even if it involves shifting the energy map of the body you apply.

An Anatomy of Energy Bodies

If you look at an acupuncture point map, you may notice certain points along the body that correspond with the chakras. A chakra, from the Sanskrit *cakra* or "wheel," signifies an energy point on the body. Each point acts as an intersection of the flow of energies within the body. We borrow this image from Tibetan and Yogic practices because it offers a lot of useful ways to categorize incidents that affect physical and spiritual bodies together. On a physical level, we see them as nerve clusters. On an energetic level, they manifest as moving wheels of energy that keep our emotional, mental, spiritual, and physical conduits flowing. For most people, the emotional body presses tightly to the physical body. When we respond to something on a visceral level, we normally feel it from the physical and emotional body combined, which is why certain emotions may make our heart beat faster or our stomach knot with anxiety. Next is the mental body, where thoughts, impressions, and images are formed from the information gathered by our physical and emotional bodies. Finally is the astral body, the one that generates magick, connects to the spiritual world, and filters our inner and outer perceptions. When people read auras, they usually discern the astral body.

Symptoms of Common Injuries to the Energetic Bodies

Our energy bodies often take damage along with our physical bodies. Like our physical bodies, they also have an immune system for repair and protection. However, this healing can become more difficult if we are subjected to destructive energies repeatedly. Just as remaining in a dirty and cluttered environment can give us more health issues over time, remaining in an unhealthy psychological environment can degrade our energetic hardiness. Hexes and curses exploit this vulnerability by disrupting natural healing processes. The better you understand the types of injuries hexes and curses cause, the more you can move beyond them.

Clogged Chakras

Healthy chakras spin at a constant rate. However, when subjected to too much of the wrong kind of energy, they get clogged and become sluggish. The cause of congestion is usually physical. For example, a person with a lethargic solar plexus chakra may have heartburn. A simple change of habit—stop eating foods that cause heartburn—can set that energy to rights. But other times, such internal encumbrance can come from outside sources.

When someone conducts a concentrated psychic attack, it appears and feels different from a single-source chakra clog. A person may experience concentrated pain and stabbing sensations directly in the chakra region or feel disoriented, despite medical tests showing the physical body functioning normally.

Daily physical exercises, such as any gym workout, clear gunk from our chakras almost as well as they do from our bodies. Even so, determined attackers may repeat their intrusions until they sense results. In the most extreme cases, the result can be damage to the physical body as much as the energetic body.

Aura Holes

Over the years, I have met multiple people with holes in their auras. Almost every single person shrugs and says, "I can't repair this; it's just a problem I have to live with." *This assumption is not true!* While I do not wish to victim blame, I want to stress that we live in a universe made of neutral energy. When a tear happens in our fields, we can find something that *will* repair it.

Tears and holes are relatively easy to identify. They often come as a sensation, usually pain: one spot on the body feels too hot or too cold. It may feel like a burn or bruise despite no markings on the skin. You may have a sense of something feeling a little too open. If an astral parasite has attached, the energy may feel like it has a sort of bump or curve in it that does not match the physical body's shape. In particularly bad cases, such tears can damage the mental body. People with auric holes may find they pick up others' thoughts and energies too easily as they go about their daily lives.

Holes can happen by accident, but the majority come from willful psychic attacks. For example, when someone creates a poppet for malicious purposes, the pins or hooks tear through energy layers. Through these holes, bad energy enters the target. The hole is held open with the pin. Our energetic bodies also have self-healing systems that form scabs and repair naturally, but the pin interferes with this process. Simply put, this is how a poppet/ pin spell can damage. Used against you, it can become a powerful weapon in your favor, as you will see in a later chapter.

Random astral parasites may sense vulnerability and dig through the layers of our auras for food. These infections happen most in energetically unkempt spaces, especially those that see a lot of foot traffic. Movie theaters, shopping malls, and doctor's offices tend to carry astral germs to the same degree that they carry the type identifiable with a microscope.

The most severe psychic attacks come from psychic vampires and angry magick workers. Psychic vampires in and of themselves are not a black-and-white issue; those that find ways to manage their needs operate ethically and consume prana (life force energy) from consensual and ambient sources. Most psychic vampires feed by placing a cord from their energy bodies into the food source. In especially vicious attacks, they infiltrate the spinal cord and internal organs. The cord drains energy from the target, leaving that person open to all sorts of infections, illnesses, and influences.

In most cases, burning away the vampire cords and creating energetic blocks between the victim and the vampire will stop the attack. After such an attack, the victim needs massive healing. People do not recover on their own from deep vampire attacks. If this happens, seek out a Reiki healer or a psychic vampire of sound moral practice for help. For those who catch minor entity attachments easily, a daily and weekly practice of cord-cutting and fire cleansing can greatly reduce these incidents and their severity.

How to Identify and Repair Aura Holes

Newer practitioners may not have an innate knowledge of how to detect energy clogs and entity attachments. The awareness comes with time and practice. If you lack psychic sensitivity, having a friend use a pendulum or visiting a Reiki healer can help you find and repair some spots in your energy bodies. However, I offer these modifications for solitary and secret practitioners, so that you can give yourself some care until you find the exact right help you need.

THE POPPET MAP

A poppet (effigy) symbolically links the doll to a person. You can make a poppet of yourself to help identify and repair damages to your energy body—you don't even need to sew! Draw two dolls of yourself: a basic paper doll like the kind people cut out to make paper chains works fine. Choose one side to represent the front of the body and the other the back. Using a crayon, outline each energy body on the poppet. Then, sketch the seven primary chakras. The big seven are: one at your tailbone, one in your reproductive region, one just above your belly, one in your heart, in the center of your throat, in the middle of your forehead, and one roughly a foot above your head. Write your name, birth date, and anything else you consider important about yourself on the back. Your doll is now ready for diagnostics! For those newer to the practice, use a pendulum and hover over each chakra, watching for the pendulum to say yes or make a jerking motion midswing on any areas that have damage or need repair.

THE BODY SCAN MEDITATION

The following meditation technique has many applications in magickal work. All you need do is sit or stand still, close your eyes, and mentally feel your way through your body. First, assess your emotional state: Do you feel good or bad today? Next, starting at your feet and working your way up, feel around for areas of discomfort—tight muscles, injuries, other areas of pain. Then look for untroubled spots on your body. As you become more skilled, you can then move from scanning your physical body to your mental and emotional body. Are there any lingering areas of concern in your chakras? As you become more skilled at this meditation, your awareness of your body and mood alignment will also improve. After some time, you can easily find the areas of yourself that may have damage and need some assistance to heal.

Repairing Damage

Some injuries may prove easier to mend than others. Usually, small auric injuries heal in one or two sessions. Often after healing a small wound, you end up wondering if you even *had* that injury and may have no idea how you got it. You will often know exactly how and when you got larger injuries. Most of the worst damage happens at a time of physical trauma, such as a broken bone from a car accident.

Most aura injuries do not come from hexing and cursing. They are often a byproduct of an emotional event combined with a physical one and are most prone to happen when someone does not fully express emotions. Life by itself offers enough trauma without extra help. The injury's origin only matters if the sustained injury is itself a curse because the curse may interfere with energetic and physical healing processes.

Recipe: Tissue Repair Tea

This tea works well to heal energetic wounds. Crafted from herbs that either lower stress or repair bodily tissue, it is useful as either a tea or a smoke-cleaning mix.

YOU WILL NEED:

   1 t comfrey root

   1 t calendula

   ½ t Solomon's seal

   1 t teasel

Mix the herbs in a one-cup-capacity jar. Steep one tablespoon of tea in hot water for seven minutes. Sweeten with natural sugars. Drink up to three cups daily for seven days. Monitor the tea's effect by using a pendulum on your poppet map or by checking with a body scan once a day. Herbal formulas tend to have a slow, subtle effect, so do not expect immediate relief.

Starstuff Repair

Back when I first began practice, I did not draw from the earth's energy for shielding. Instead, I drew from the stars themselves; at the time, it felt more natural to me. Over the years, I found more ways to ground to the earth, so I have done this less. Even so, especially if you can't get to a Reiki healer in the nick of time, getting that healing energy from the stars can work wonders.

Find a place you can sit without anyone disturbing you. Do not use headphones. While normally they are useful for blocking distractions, sounds are important in this case. Put your phone in another room. Settle yourself in a comfortable place, preferably sitting on the floor (on a pillow is fine). Listen to the ambient noise around you, noticing how every noise vibrates. Let the movement fill you. As you feel yourself filling with atomic motion, imagine everything around you melting away. See yourself floating in the universe amidst a field of stars as their vibrations meld with your body. As you stay in this state, the various holes and patches in your energy bodies will fill as the starlight burns away any parasitic attachments. What remains will, if desired, meld with you.

Once you feel like you've taken all you need, thank the stars, and imagine the solid world returning. Wiggle your fingers and toes, stand up, move around, and then go about your ordinary day.

Burns

Psychic burns tend to happen when someone engages in a direct magickal battle. If this happened, you would know exactly why your body hurt. While other psychic burns based on energetic "allergies" have happened to some people, they are rare.

My direct experience comes from catching both hellfire and holy fire burns at different times, not from any battle, but as a result of the attached entities who were trying to help me burn something off that wasn't supposed to be there. Even celestial and infernal beings sometimes have shaky hands.

They both hurt, but in different ways. If scorched by hellfire, which happens when a demon burns you, it feels like sunstroke. Holy fire feels more like touching a hot oven without a mitt. In both cases, you may experience elevated body temperature and a skin rash. Treat psychic burns just as you would a physical burn: hydrate heavily, put aloe and ice packs where you feel the injury, and rest. If possible, avoid situations where you may end up physically burned by a supernatural being. The best way to do this is to just not engage in magickal attack scenarios. If it is unavoidable for you, however, you at least now know what first aid applies.

Spirit Attachments

Spirit and entity attachments used to happen with far less frequency than they do now. Why it occurs more now probably speaks to a collective absence of self-care. The level of danger posed by them depends on the carrier and how the spirit attached in the first place. In most situations, it's a mild parasitic attachment that functions much the same as a tick. While the parasite may not drain you altogether, every so often you get one that carries a disease or pathogen that can really mess you up. In those cases, you may need the help of someone sensitive enough to spot the critter. You have to extract the attachment, trap it in something, and heal and seal the energetic wound beneath. Disposal of the trapped entity should come after the healing. Do not try to simply release an entity attachment outside unless guided to do so, as it is most likely to return to its original host and reattach. Worse, it may find a new host with less defenses than the original.

The following is a simple parasite extraction method I use regularly.

YOU WILL NEED:

A glass of water

Two straws cut from a small broom

An egg

A sage bundle

Copal or frankincense incense

A sealing oil such as olive oil or myrrh

Set the glass of water next to you and the person with the attachment. Cut two straws from the broom and place them next to the glass. Take the egg and roll it over the area with the attachment. Typically, an astral bug feels like a weight or something that hangs off the body. As you roll the egg, imagine the energies merging and the egg forming an umbilical cord to the attachment. Jerk the egg and see/feel the attachment entering it. Immediately drop the egg, still in the shell, in the glass of water. Place the broom straws across the top of the glass. Use the sage bundle to cleanse the person and follow up with copal or frankincense to seal off their energy and prevent reentry. Complete the process by anointing the target's head, hands, and feet with an oil such as Crown of Success.

To finish, remove the broom straws and flush the egg down the toilet. Throw the water, broom straws, and jar at a crossroads. Do not look back to where you threw it. Something will come and take it home.

Soul Loss

Soul loss can happen in this lifetime or throughout several incarnations. A person with soul loss is spiritually ill and, if the condition is exacerbated, stops wanting things that nourish their soul. They often put needs before wants to the point of near self-sacrifice and gradually neglect all but the basest needs over time. They may give too much of themselves to others or simply dive into an addiction. If this sounds like co-dependence and/or depression, these conditions often but do not always exist alongside soul-loss.

Most people living in the industrial world suffer from a certain lack of spiritual nourishment to some degree. If possible, seek out a shaman or attend workshops on soul retrieval—the process takes a lot of work but is well worth recovering and healing your fragmented energy. Chapter ten discusses the topic in more detail.

Magickal Cleansing: Getting the Ick Off

These days, most people know that waving a little burning white sage (either *Salvia apiana* or *Artemisia ludoviciana*) around can remove large chunks of bad energy. This common knowledge is good; it's a handy go-to technique for clearing things out. But it is also bad because the people who send negative energy most often also know about sage and likely use it. Given the absolute fluidity with which someone can craft magickal energy, it is entirely possible to craft sage-resistant workings. Not only can some people switch sage to the "off" position, but certain entities also find sage annoying and even enraging.

Baths

A magickal bath need not happen in a bathtub. It does, however, require water. There are four general approaches people take to spiritual bathing: the first is to kneel in the tub and pour water over the head, the second is to have a good soak, the third is to prepare an oil scrub of salt and herbs to rub over the body and the head, and the last is to prepare a bowl of water or milk with herbs added that the person then pours over their head. While I prefer a good soak, any of these methods can work.

Recipe: Bath Scrub

To prepare your general cleansing bath, try this recipe.

YOU WILL NEED:

   1 C Epsom salt

   1 C sea salt

   ½ C of Hawaiian black salt

1 C olive or sunflower oil (or any other skin-safe carrier oil)

Quart jar

Mix the salts in a bowl. Add the carrier oil a little bit at a time, stirring until the mixture forms a paste. Spoon the paste into a glass jar. Use this as a body scrub or add to your bathwater as a spiritual cleansing go-to.

Smoke Cleansing

To perform a smoke cleansing on yourself, you need either a dried herb bundle that you can keep in a heatproof container or a stick of incense that you can snuff out. To cleanse yourself or another person with smoke, light the bundle or the incense. Pass the incense over the bottom of each foot, then around the outline of your body. When you complete the outline, start at the top of the head and move downward, rolling the smoke around the body in a circle. Make sure to circle both legs and both arms. If performing this on yourself, you may need to use both hands to pass the incense very carefully around your body.

Egg Cleansing

A detailed explanation of egg cleansing is in the previous chapter. This method is also useful for general cleansing, not only for looking for curses. Take a room temperature egg and roll it over the body, starting at the crown of the head. Make sure to roll down the inside of the arms and legs and over the bottom of the feet. If you drop the egg, grab another egg and start again from the beginning. When finished, set the egg down in a place it can't roll away, anoint yourself with protection or sealing oil, and speak a prayer to seal your aura against any intrusion.

Candle/Fire Cleansing

Light a white Shabbat candle and run the flame about one to two inches above the skin, from head to toe. Do not do this naked. It can burn out certain invisible critters that might hang on to you.

Potion Cleansing

A potion is a liquid intended for either ingestion or as something you add to bathwater. For this, I am recommending you make a simple tea composed of three to seven edible cleansing or spell breaking herbs. Ingestion should help cleanse your energy bodies of any intrusive material without serious intestinal side effects.

If you are uncertain where to begin with a cleansing, try the following potion first.

Recipe: Energy Cleansing Potion

This simple tonic allows your aura a gentle reset over the course of a few days. You can drink as is, but it tastes more than a little odd. If you want to brew this, preserve it in vodka, and then add ten drops of the tincture to your preferred beverage (or even a sports drink); it works just as well in sodas as it does in fruit juice. You may even want to look at the folkloric associations of the drink you mix it in to see if it can enhance your results.

YOU WILL NEED:

1 T dried lemon peel

1 t hyssop

1 t mugwort

1 t lemongrass

A pinch of rosemary

A pinch of sea salt

A dash of flax, cow, or goat milk

Boil water in a tea kettle. While the water heats, pack the dried herbs into a tea strainer. When the water reaches boiling, pour into a heatproof cup, and add the dried herbs and sea salt. Allow to steep for 7 to 10 minutes. Add a dash of milk, stir, and drink. Sweeten to taste.

Earth Cleansing

Earthing is the easiest and most delightful of all cleansing methods. All you need to do is go outdoors. If you feel you have more negative energy on you than you can carry, go outside and lie on the nearest low-traffic patch of earth. Start on your back, looking upward, and when you feel that has cleared, roll over onto your stomach and allow any further energy to soak into the soil. Seal off the work by hugging a tree, which will exchange its energy for yours, setting you both a bit more right.

Aura Cleansing Ingredients

A host of ingredients clean the body and spirit, most of which are affordable and available at any grocery store. Seasoned practitioners tend to keep these in stock at home and then use them in a mix and match of recipes as needed. I think the most thorough cleansings cover at least the five Western elements. You blow off the light stuff (air), burn off the heavy stuff (fire), wash off the deeper stuff (water), and ground out the worst stuff (earth). You may finish with a prayer asking to seal off all the roads between you and the path through which the stuff got to you (spirit). The following is a list of common occult cleansing substances and how to apply them. These items can cleanse your body, wash your laundry, or serve as household cleaners.

Epsom Salt

Pouring one cup in bathwater removes most nastiness from your person. Add to your laundry-prewash cycle to remove persistent energies from your clothing.

Water

Water cleanses, freezes, and drowns. Whether from the shower or the sink, you can use it to wash away trouble or halt a problem by grabbing a jinxed object and freezing it. Need more space in your freezer? Dust it with some spell breaker powder and then leave it outside to melt.

Florida Water

This popular spiritual cologne available at botanicas and Latin American grocery stores leaves a fresh scent as it gives anything it touches a potent cleansing. Pour it in spray bottles and spritz in areas and over objects in lieu of smoke cleansing.

Shabbat Candles (White)

You can find white Shabbat candles in supermarkets, near the prepackaged matzo ball soup. While intended for honoring Jewish Shabbat, these basic white candles come in handy for removing negative energies through fire cleansing or candle pulling. Candle pulling is a way to remove negative energy by circling the candle over someone's crown chakra, thus pulling out the negative energy. The candle is then burned to dispose of the bad energy.

Colloidal Silver

This silver-infused water washes away some of the most resistant energies, especially those from shadow energies or unfriendly faeries. Colloidal silver mixes well into most energy-clearing sprays. Most people can get it from the health and beauty aisle of higher-end grocery stores.

Iron Powder

Iron powder has vast protective properties; not only can it block out unfriendly faeries, but it also forms a sort of weapon energy in potions and oils. The presence of iron adds longevity to the protective charge in any formula. You may have to order the powder from an occult shop if you do not happen to know someone who works at a steel mill.

Magnets

Magnets can pull things in, push them away, and block things. They are extremely useful in redirecting problematic energies. Magnetized hematite works wonders in pulling deep-set energies out of all bodies. Refrigerator magnets may not work their magick as dramatically, but they do work.

Alum Crystal

You can find this powder with the pickling spices at any grocery store. Used as a souring preservative and a quick way to treat shaving cuts, this mineral has immediate clearing energy. Its sour taste makes it a go-to component of gossip stopping spells.

Cleansing Herbs

Cleansing herbs can overlap with the next section, spell breaker herbs. Cleansers for the most part work differently from spell breakers. They take off general "dirt" that adds to sensations of heaviness and stagnation in most people, whereas breakers overwrite and erase any intentions. There is no set formula for any of these herbs; combinations can depend on your understanding of how the herb works with the human body (whether ingested or externally applied) and any animistic relationships developed with a given plant or group of plants. The following list gives a general idea of what the herb can help with and how it reacts. If marked for internal use, the substance is safe to ingest.

LAVENDER
Internal and external; clearing communication issues, reducing stressors, sweetening soured situations.

LEMONGRASS
Internal and external; clearing, creating optimism.

EUCALYPTUS
Internal and external; clarity, removal of stagnation.

CEDAR
External; repels pests metaphorically and physically.

LEMON
Internal and external; clarity, mood-lifting, calming in combination with other herbs.

LIME
Internal and external; clarity, mood-lifting, complex banishing (can reach deeper layers than lemon), absorption of negative energies.

GARLIC SKIN
External; exorcism effect that drives off energies and entities.

ONION SKIN
External; when burned, has mild exorcism/phytoremediation effect of absorbing and transmuting energies.

SOLOMON'S SEAL
External; as an oil, ingredient expels energies. When burned, acts as an exorcism on spirits and banishes abstractions such as financial debt.

BALM OF GILEAD
External; oil-soluble, applied as a healing balm for skin concerns; burned removes "stuck" energy through lubrication.

WORMWOOD
External; do not burn. As a vinegar, tincture clears away physical pests and astral parasites.

ANGELICA
External and internal; boosts a "light" energy effect that makes a tense/stuffy atmosphere feel lighter.

BAY LAUREL
External and internal; burned does double duty by clearing energy and leaving protection behind; ingested can assist with mental clarity and makes a delicious flavoring for chicken dishes.

SULFUR
External only; drives off low-grade pests, pairs well as a fertilizer for air-cleansing house plants. When wet, creates signal confusion

for demonic energies. Burn for banishment. Only use wet if prepared for drunken demons.

CHICORY
Internal and external; operates both physically and spiritually as a potent diuretic.

COFFEE
Internal, clarity, and clarification; external, delivers exorcism with force.

CHAPARRAL
External; clears energy and offers an opportunity to rewrite negative energy into any intention desired when burned. Use requires cultivation of a relationship with the plant.

GREEN TEA
Internal; gentle clarity and restores calm.

HYSSOP
Internal and external; removes psychic debris and calms more extreme home disturbances.

TOBACCO
External; exorcises spirits and leaves a layer of protection behind. Tobacco only works reliably when burned in herb form; cigarette additives make results unpredictable.

KUDZU VINE (ALT: CREEPING CHARLIE)
External; burned or as an alcohol-based spray energetically overwhelms whatever it is aimed at. While in the physical world it chokes/overwhelms, taken internally it clears/eases breathing—

the metaphor can apply to energetically clogged atmospheres and places where pollution creeps in.

LEMON BALM
Internal; soothing clarity, calms anxiety severe enough to be felt in the environment.

MATÉ
Internal and external creates gentle clarity, also blocks stagnation and hostility from returning. When ingested, allows a sense of calm alertness.

MUGWORT
Internal and external; settles disturbed conditions; soothes anxiety.

NEEM
External; acts as a potent exorcism and prevents reinvasion.

PENNYROYAL
External, removes mid-grade stagnant energy; internally, acts as a purgative of negativity. Do not use while pregnant.

ROSEMARY
Internal and external; clarity, when burned, clears energy like a bay leaf.

ROSE
External; petals act as absorbers; thorns pierce and break down servitors/sent energies; a wash made from the leaves restores inner peace after long periods of difficulty.

CARNATION

External and internal; petals absorb and transmute negative energy into positive.

BASIL

External and internal; improves clarity and increases other herbs' potency in a formula with it, whether burned or ingested.

Spell Breakers

Sometimes you just have a spell on you or something in your home. If you do, you probably want that spell off you, pronto! Magickal folk are always inventing and reprogramming their energy constructions, so while the list below gives a general overview, nothing in the list applies to every situation.

AMMONIA—LIQUID AND POWDERED

A little bit of baker's ammonia sprinkled on a bespelled object often acts as an off switch to magickal intentions. When I worked at a magick shop with a coworker overly fond of throwing down small jinxes for the other employees, I spent a lot of time just brushing bits of powder over her energy trail. Often people would comment on the overwhelming brightness of the shop after I finished my work. Ammonia is very effective, but its power comes with a price—it clears away everything—protection and prosperity work included.

MYRRH

Myrrh tree gum resin has a wonderful way of bending and blending into the other material you mix with it. It does wonderful double duty as an astringent cleanser. Demons do not fare well with myrrh; they often react worse to this than they do to rue.

Burn a little if you believe someone hired mischief out to certain sulfur-loving spirits.

RUE

Rue is a finicky plant that won't work with everyone but it's a wunderkind if it likes you. It acts as protection, reversal, cleanser, and banisher. Like myrrh, it can interweave its energy with just about any other plant for a nuanced result. Before you burn or wash it, talk with it about what's going on and listen. Often it gives those it allies with tips on how to get the most out of it. Despite coming from a different part of the world, rue pairs especially well with eucalyptus for reversals and spell breaking works.

EUCALYPTUS

While eucalyptus is popular as an essential oil, its use in leaf form is often overlooked. Eucalyptus does a wonderful job of breaking down outside intentions. Entities and energies that resist sage can be banished with eucalyptus smoke.

Improving Metaphysical Immunity

Certain people—usually empaths—can't seem to leave the house without catching some metaphysical astral bug. My running theory as to why this happens is that most empaths have their emotional bodies on the outside. I will delve more into this concept in chapter four. If you are among those who "catch" things easily, the following small steps can reduce time on cleansings.

Head Covering

Some magick practitioners wear scarves and turbans as symbols of their faith and commitment. Others prefer hats. I get too warm with hats and prefer to minimize overt occult signaling, so I wear a barrette or hairpin I blessed when I am not teaching magick. When heading into an especially fraught area, like the closed asylum near my home, I also hide a single braid within the layers of my hair as a way of filtering the psychic information that reaches me.

Gloves

When spirit workers lay tricks—spells meant for others, usually via a powder, spray, or object—they put them in places they know their victims will touch. Gloves, especially those with lace and knotwork, can slow down what you might absorb that way.

Protection Oil/Perfume

I encourage people to wear a protection oil daily. Anointing the body or an object with a magical oil has a cumulative effect. It helps build and strengthen energy shields. If fragrance or allergies pose a problem, simply pray over a little olive oil and use that.

Protect Shoes and Feet

Some negative spells activate when the target walks across them. Place a little Devil's Shoestring oil in your shoe to break any spells you may step on.

Hide Protections

There are magickal folks who wear their faith and protection symbols to signal who they are and what they do to other workers and their clients. The practice works well in communities that support these magickal folks and their trade, but sometimes the less people who know about you and how you protect yourself, the better. When I do wear those charms, I pin them inside my clothing. If a would-be attacker knows your defenses, they can plan to knock them down. The less someone knows about what you use, the better.

Hide Your Eyes

Some practitioners recommend wearing sunglasses in photos because the eyes are a window to the soul, making their inner magick trove easy to access for the determined. I prefer not to hide my eyes, so I indulge my vanity instead. I borrow from the Egyptian tradition of lining the eyes to prevent any energetic intrusion while increasing my gaze's projective power. In times past, hiding from photos made most of this unnecessary. Today, we have less choice. We live in a society where an absence of photos of yourself decreases trust in you; it's hard to avoid having your picture taken. While hiding eyes can reduce another's ability to work magickal harm on you, it can also do practical harm if a potential employer wants to get a feel for you.

Sigils on the Skin

Draw sigils on your skin in hidden places. Like any charm or spell, sigils have a shelf life. Make a point of drawing fresh ones in hidden places each day such as between your fingers. The practice of changing symbols and where they adorn you gives any would-be attackers moving targets—it's hard to aim your energy at someone with constantly changing defenses.

Identifying Energy Bodies

While some people may have larger energetic bodies than others and some people have energetic bodies larger than their physical bodies, those forms all have the same function.

The list here shows the standard order of energetic bodies:

1. Physical body

2. Emotional body

3. Mental body

4. Auric body

People with this arrangement align with what Western medicine classifies as neurotypical.

For those with energy bodies in "normal" order, the business of cleansing is straightforward. Scrubbing, cutting ties, and shielding the auric body resolves most issues. But needs change for people with energy bodies and chakras in a different order. If you try cleansing methods that people swear by to no avail or shielding never seems to work for you, you may have a different energy body order than commonly assumed. Empaths and psychic vampires especially struggle with standard cleansing and clearing methods not having the needed effect.

Determining Energy Body Order

The standard method of determining basic energy bodies' order relies on a talent called psychometry. In psychometry, a person senses unseen energy through touch. While this talent is reasonably common, not everyone has this ability. At this time, I am working on diagnostic methods for people that do not have psychometry but those methods are not ready for publication just yet. The psychometry method works by putting your hands close to or far from someone as specific energy moves through their bodies. First, obtain permission to touch the person you want to examine. I rarely need to touch anyone to perform this diagnostic, but for the extremely sensitive, touching their energy fields is the same as touching their body. I ask the person to think of a multiplication table. I then bring my hands in toward their body and stop when I feel a sense of motion. Finding out where they generate motion when thinking of something analytical like math shows me the location of the mental body. Next, I ask them to think of something that makes them laugh and move my hands to where I can sense that movement. For a person with a neurotypical order, the laughter brings me close to the physical body. For empaths, however, I sense the laughter sometimes as far away as ten feet from the physical body.

The manner in which to care for energy bodies in atypical order varies for each person. The nuances of those needs extend beyond the scope of countermagick. For now, be conscious that if you are an empath, you need to shield your emotional body in addition to shielding your auric body. If you have your mental body on the outside, you may need to practice a triple-shield.

The world has far more inhabiting it than simply empaths, vampires, and the "normal." We are still discovering new aspects of our physical bodies every day, which is far more than we know about our energy forms. Just as mainstream medicine works first with what it knows and builds from there, so do those of us attempting to understand the spiritual and physiological. When it comes to working with these bodies in a cursing context, knowing about them improves cleansing practices drastically and gives us better ways to defend ourselves.

For now, remember that you need to clean yourself—even behind your ears—to get metaphysical and physical ick off. Always cleanse yourself first. Remember that the better you know your body and its orders, the better you can manage and disperse any negative energies that find you.

FOUR

AH! GET IT OUT OF HERE!
Driving Negative Magick Out of the Home

When someone determined to attack you wants a specific result, they typically don't mess with your person alone. They attack anywhere you consider home. They may lay tricks (negative spells activated by contact with you) at your workplace, in your car, and, if they know where you live, at your doorstep. Why do it this way? Because when you want to take someone down, you hit them where they live. When these attackers hit you, they also find ways to make sure you know it.

Even the psychically nonsensitive can sometimes recognize a home under cursing/psychic attack. Rooms feel like a violent argument has lingered, even if no one in the house quarreled that day. The air feels heavy and out of sync with weather conditions.

Hangout spots feel itchy or uncomfortable for no traceable reason. Sometimes poltergeist-like activity happens with items seeming to jump off shelves and lights flickering.

When these conditions occur, it's a warning but *not* a guarantee of cursing/psychic attack. Suppose a curse, not emotional conflict within the dwelling residents, is the cause. In that case, the goal is to create a toxic energetic environment intended to lead to the target's total breakdown. Left unchecked or ignored, these bad energies really can degrade someone's quality of life. Homes filled with people committed to principles of peace and respect can usually protect themselves with ease. They simply have to reaffirm the values of their home and use magickal cleansing tools to reinforce those values. Homes founded on poor communication and negativity may not notice a curse because it sneaks in on the back of the poor values, and thus it becomes all the more difficult to identify and remove badness that has wormed its way in.

How Clutter Lets Bad Energy Stick

Remember that old saw about cleanliness being next to godliness? If godliness means too slippery to let gross energy stick, sure, we can call it that. Dust particles tend to carry tiny essences of other energies, and dust particles get in anywhere without a hermetic seal. Even if you close your living space and allow no entry for twenty years, dust and bugs will find their way in. The dust mite is the avatar of entropy.

People who engage in spiritual attacks often align their energies with chaos to do so. If they don't have direct energetic ties, they can always access our atmosphere's dust and dirt. When the dust settles, it becomes stagnant. The lack of ambient motion eventually inundates you with muck and poisons your whole life.

There are two techniques commonly used to banish gener-alized negative energy: sage and sweep. These serve best when you don't need to know where the ick came from or when you just want to get it out so you can feel comfortable in your space. Before you run for your sage, however, please consider some less-known information about its long-term use in magickal practice.

Why Sage Sometimes Makes Problems Worse

Some magick workers grab sage as their go-to at the earliest sign of negative energy. Most of the time, it works brilliantly, How-ever, like all things magickal, the plant has limits. Sage moves out emotionally charged energies and can persuade some—but not all—spirits to move on. For the most part, it banishes the atmo-spheric traces of unpleasant human emotions. It does *not* banish every type of spirit, only certain types. The spirits it does not banish tend to be the sort that pose more immediate danger to someone having an energy issue.

Some may wonder at this point why I no longer use the phrase "smudging" to refer to the purposeful burning of sage. While many nations/tribes do burn white sage, smudging itself is a spe-cific ritual that varies from group to group. This ritual is not shared with people outside of the tribe or family, making it a closed prac-tice. While non-Native people who have not been taught a smudg-ing ceremony do cleanse with white sage, the practice simply isn't smudging. Multiple conversations with native people, including my own partner, have made it clear that there isn't one singular smudging practice—and thus I can't call it that anymore based on my own ethics.

I also want to mention that burning an herb alone does not always result in a cleansing, or may only yield partial success. If you have not built a relationship with that plant, you may not experience its full benefit. I chose to work with prairie white sage (not popular when I adopted it) because I lived in an area with a storied history of indigenous people and spirits, and sage was a native plant to that area that those spirits understood and responded well to. It made sense to me to build a relationship with a plant that connected to that history. Before I burned the plant, I talked to it. When possible, I grew it. I did not just start using it without so much as a polite introduction.

Over the years, I found certain spirits unaffected or sometimes enraged by white sage smoke. It does nothing to persuade a djinn to move on. Some faeries merely find the smoke annoying. If someone summons a demon, the sage may even feed it. For general reference, this is what both types of white sage work for:

- Removing lingering emotional imprints.
- Spirits of the dead, with limitations based on the strength of that spirit.
- General "sticky" debris that comes from interaction with other people.

What white sage does *not* work for:

- Removing living spirits, e.g., faeries, demons, or similar entities.
- Removing a viral/built entity such as a servitor.
- Itself—if someone wove white sage into their working, they have inoculated themselves against your go-to clearing method.

It's always a bad idea to over-rely on one tool in magickal practice, and sage may be the most overused of magickal tools when I write this. Fortunately, you have scores of other methods and materials to explore when it comes to cleansing your house and aligning your energy.

Sweeping

Sweeping removes negative energy by gathering up the dust and moving it out. Intentional sweeping works well on general miasma, especially after a period of illness.

When you sweep, be sure to clear both dust bunnies (look under your bed!) and spiderwebs first. Both can act as little energy bombs or land mines. Once you remove those, start in on more stubborn areas. Make sure you get the corners of every room; underneath beds, desks, couches, and bureaus; and, if possible, clean off your closet floors. Some folk traditions call you to start at the back of your house and sweep forward, sending out all the bad energy through the front door. Afterward, pour buckets of water on your front step (if feasible) to wash the bad away. Using a garden hose is an acceptable labor-saving move in this case. If you live in an apartment building, you may do this with the entrance to your apartment or the driveway entrance if your building has a shared parking lot. After you sweep, follow up by sealing the energy. You can do this by burning a resin incense such as dragon's blood or anointing the doors and windows with a tiny dot of prayed-over olive oil.

Treat your cleaning tools with the same sanctity you hold for any tools of the magickal craft. Some witches like to burn their brooms twice a year to start with a sweeping tool fresh at each solstice. If this seems wasteful to you, cleaning your broom with soap and water and following with a little bit of Florida Water should keep it in spiritually clean condition.

Sweeping, unlike smoke cleansing, works entirely in the three-dimensional plane. However, it cannot remove material left in the astral, nor can it remove anything created to bridge material and spiritual dimensions. Know the benefits of your practice…and its limits.

Is It a Spell or a Spirit?

To rid your space of stubborn energies and entities, it helps to identify them. When determining what that is, you may obsess about the identity of the sender. You may panic at what you find— "Oh no, a demon!" Or, you may never know exactly what it was. Even if what you find seems horrifying, keep an open mind. In most cases, every spirit encounter presents an opportunity to make an ally.

Using divination for diagnostics can help with identifying a spirit. While there are no hard and fast rules about what might represent a spirit or spell in the tarot, often the Magician, High Priestess, and the 7 of Cups represent a spell; almost any of the court cards can indicate a spirit or the person sending the energy. However, servitors may be harder to spot because they tend to work like viruses—neither alive nor dead, they don't always register until you know what feeds them or how someone made them. If servitors are a persistent issue, you may want to designate your own divination for identifying them.

Identifying Negative Energy Sources

For the most effective warding and sealing of your home, account for every layer of reality for openings through which undesired energies can enter. Yes, dust and corners always gather negative energy thanks to their static nature. So do shadowy spots. Doors, windows, and stairs are prone to spiritual traffic.

Mirrors can be very tricky and can serve as portals or wards, depending on how you treat them. Maintain excellent cleaning and warding practices with anything reflective because just washing fingerprints off a mirror with an ammonia-based cleaner can open a spiritual highway into your house if you're not vigilant. Ammonia acts as a super-cleanser that takes down any energy in its path, including wards you set yourself. Because of its aggressive nature, intention makes no difference whatsoever—even spilling ammonia will wipe out any magickal protections or structures it touches.

A cleaning practice can improve your overall life quality and offset attacks, both spiritually and emotionally. The following checklist is intended to help you keep an eye out for places in your home prone to energy stickiness that allows curse energy to stick.

NEGATIVITY CHECK

- Look for the dusty spots: bookshelves, under your bed, in back closets.

- Look for the spots that fall in shadow often: shadows allow for certain beings and energies, good and bad, to travel.

- Look at your mirrors—if you cleaned them, did you ward them?

- What is stagnant? The furniture you haven't moved in years, items you've left out for months on end, clothing you haven't worn. Move and remove as much as you can.

Decluttering has the added benefit of inviting prosperity and wealth to replace the former clogged energy.

- Check all entry doors on your dwelling—dust above the doorways.
- Wash light switches, dust light bulbs and lamp tops, and clear out dead bugs.

Sometimes we trot out all our best warding methods and it *still* takes us by surprise when things get in or won't clear despite rolling up our sleeves and scrubbing. It's often just a matter of persistence and strength on the sender's part, not a failing of our own. Some practitioners are just more robust and can brute force their way through. Even the most experienced magick workers sometimes run into loopholes in their wards and rules of entry. Before you ward in earnest, you need to understand how the non-compatible vibes found their way into your home. This checklist can help you think through your wards and the conditions you place on them, and it can help you spot any objects best chucked in the trash.

SOURCES OF ENTRY

- What has been gifted to you recently? How about gifts from people no longer in your life? Any packages "misdelivered" to your house lately?
- What does your welcome mat say? Words have power, and if it says welcome all, you might just be undercutting yourself. Perhaps switch to a mat that says "Go away." Better yet, switch to a mat with an image or phrase that only makes sense to you and your family.

- What spirits have you warded against, exactly? Many people might not, for instance, think to ward against djinn or fairies, but both sets of spirits can cause trouble unless you acknowledge them and set boundaries.

- When a guest visits your home, what do you do to clean out their energy after leaving?

- Examine your floorboards and wainscoting. Are there loose boards and dividing lines creating physical cracks that can also serve as reality cracks?

- Examine the structure of your house—odd geometries and even alignment with power lines can turn a house into an inadvertent crossroads. Crossroads tend to have high volumes of spirit traffic.

Basic House Cleansing and Warding

I have used the following cleansing and warding method for over twenty years. The effects of these methods last about a month. I encourage staying ahead of problems by performing a cleansing and protection renewal on the new moon and full moon, respectively and making every effort to stick to that schedule. You do not need to change the ritual based on the moon phase; the lunar energy and dark energy are the added ingredient and will work in their ways as you move through this practice. For added emphasis, you can work your protection ritual into your routine house cleaning.

YOU WILL NEED:

One broom—smaller is better, but your family broom will do, anointed with house blessing or general cleansing oil

One candle, blue or white

One spray bottle, filled with sea salt water and a dash of vodka to prevent mold

One bundle of white sage or an alternative clearing herb appropriate to your home, plus a dish to catch any ash

One stick of resin incense or similar (I prefer Fred Soll's brand frankincense incense as he designs it for multiple burns)

TO PREPARE:

Bless your broom. Anoint it with oil. Mix the sea salt and water in the spray bottle and set the sprayer dial to mist. Prepare your candle—you can learn candle dressing to optimize the effect from many sources online. When preparing your candle, think which power or being you might want to bless and protect your house, e.g., a god, saint, your ancestors, and so on. If it's a being you haven't worked with before, research appropriate offerings.

STEP 1: CLEAR THE CLUTTER

Do a brief walkthrough of your house. Throw any clutter into a box or basket to sort out later. This way, you can also walk through your house the second time without tripping on anything. Make sure you check your doors and windows for debris as well. Should you feel ambitious after this clearing, dust and vacuum. It need not be a deep clean, just enough to remove the surface dirt.

STEP 2: SWEEP IT OUT

Open a window or door at or near the front of your home. Start from the back of your home or the closest equivalent. Sweep ritually, broom not touching any surfaces. You may want to chant. My "chanting" is usually irritable and cuss-word laden. You can craft a poem or find something someone has written that speaks to your home and practice. "Out of my keep, back where you came from, out the door, you!" works well. Sweep above and below, under beds, and make sure you get all corners, windows, and that spot above your ceiling fan. I encourage you to take a moment, grab a rag, and dust the ceiling fan while you're up there. (You may want gloves and a mask.)

From that back area, drive the invisible critters out the front door or window. Admonish them to go somewhere else and give them a specific place to go. I tell them to return to the ocean to be reborn. I discovered the hard way that not giving direction resulted in neighbors with haunted houses…apparently not everyone enjoys that. If leaving a door or window cracked in the front of your house creates a security issue, you can do this work from the front to the back of the house to leave your doors locked.

STEP 3: SMOKE IT OUT
Start this round at your front door. Burn your chosen herb—sage, lavender, eucalyptus, whatever works for you—and tell the herbs what you want them to do. Since most people use white sage, I recommend telling it to push out any more stubborn energies and emotions and to summon friendly guardians from the natural world. When the bad stuff leaves, I encourage them during their walk of shame to go somewhere specific, such as a nearby river willing to take them. Move through every room. Make sure to cense the doors, windows, light bulbs, faucets, and electrical outlets. If this is your first time doing this, ensure that you smoke cleanse the inside of the refrigerator and all cabinet drawers. Yes, you also need to run a little smoke inside the washer and dryer tubs. You need not burn out the entire herb bundle. When you have completed your circuit through your home, snuff the incense out on a ceramic or glass plate. Place it in a sink or

shower until it has no heat or spark remaining. Leave a window open to allow any remaining smoke to clear. I have learned that if sage decides to spontaneously burn again after you put it out, spirit sees something that needs out NOW that sage can help with. Because of this phenomenon, it's best to leave it in the sink on a heatproof plate, where water can put out a fire, and leave the plant to do its thing from there.

STEP 4: SPRAY IT
Take your spray bottle of salt and water and move from the back of your house to the front, spritzing every window, corner, and door. Imagine it as a flowing warding wall. The water forms the moat to your castle, and the salt adds a metaphysical wall to your perimeters.

STEP 5: SEAL IT
Light your incense resin stick. Start at the back of your house. As you burn the resin, move towards your front entrance, tracing the outline of each door and window. Walk the perimeter of each room. State that you are locking out the bad and sealing in the good. Repeat this around wireless modems, as well as faucets and mirrors.

STEP 6: BLESS IT
Take your candle and place it on a bowl or plate at the activity center of your home. Some people may choose a fireplace mantle; others may opt for the stove. If you have roommates, place it in your bedroom. Light the candle and speak a prayer to your chosen spirits, asking them to protect your home and your people in all ways. Ask them also to reinforce your work and show you where you need to strengthen your protection.

STEP 7: SET BOUNDARIES

When you perform a cleansing and banishing, you get rid of most random/minor spirits and energies. However, it is unlikely all of them left. Some will remain, such as your ancestors, the land spirit beneath your building, hearth and home spirits, or spirits with whom you already had agreements. When you do the cleansing, you've gotten all the minor intruders out. Having a conversation with the remaining spirits establishes and renews agreements with those intending to stay in your home and contribute to the family's well-being.

To make this speech, stand in the middle of your household and address the spirits. Lay down your house rules. Common house rules for spirits include:

- Leave me alone when I'm sleeping.
- I must consent to any entities that enter here.
- Earn your keep by protecting the space from spells, spirits, and servitors.
- Alert the household immediately when someone's trying to break my wards.

For most people, a strong house-cleansing practice keeps the house and home protected and in order. That said, it's not a fool-proof method. The more you engage in magic, the more you may find yourself coming across other magic workers with oppositional intents. Magicians are always thinking up new ways to do things (including getting around each other), but for the person of average energetic/attention profile, maintaining this practice usually keeps all spirit-activity incidents manageable.

Advanced Warding Methods for Home

The need for warding does not stem solely from the reality of psychic attack. Sometimes the curious expose themselves to strange things in their explorations of interesting haunted places that get curious about them in turn. With preventions in place, you can keep things from following you home after your explorations.

While the above cleansing and warding practice constitutes an essential defense line, it can only defend against a specific set of commonly recognized energies. Your energy will automatically ward away (or invite in) what it knows. For example, if you work with smaller devas and nature spirits, you likely have automatic filters connecting to those you can allow in or take out.

If you don't interact much with demons or djinn, someone who knows that might send those beings in to afflict you. If you express a lot of superstition or fear of specific entities, it increases the likelihood that someone out to attack you will make use of them. If you don't fully understand the extremely broad scope of fae energy and culture, your lack of knowledge can work against you. If you have ancestors who never worked on their healing, someone can pull that thread in your life. You can't always know what causes a disturbance, and finding out can force you to expand your inner and outer worlds. Even the most psychic among us are in no way omniscient. The overview in this book comes nowhere close to exhausting the list of energies that could challenge your security protocols.

What follows is a mix of practices that can sometimes help, especially during and after a psychic attack.

1. SWITCH YOUR METHODS

Researching magickal disciplines and methods outside your tradition tends to pay off when it comes to protection. It's like switching computer operating systems to stop hacking. If standard warding doesn't work, switch to sigils. If protection candles don't work, dig up some ceremonial magick methods. Examine sacred geometry and apply those structures in your wards. Some might call this dilettantism; I call it best practice.

2. ATTEMPT TO TALK TO THE SPIRIT
There's a great deal more on this in chapter nine, but sometimes direct conversation works the best. Start off polite and firm. Based on how the communication goes, adjust your attitude. Sometimes poltergeist activity are just disputes with roommates you didn't know you had.

Magickal Data Protection
You may be trying to figure out how someone found a way to directly get at you despite your intense efforts to prevent attacks. Your wards are secure. You take extra care not to leave DNA anywhere. Hell, you drag a stick behind you everywhere you walk just to cover your tracks. Yet still, someone found a way to get at you.

In modern society, it's well nigh impossible to cover your tracks completely. Add the growing number of people who have developed psychic talent in recent decades and just assume no map exists from which you can entirely fall off. All certain people need is a name; some just need a face; others need only sense your energy, which does everything.

How Bad Spells Stick
After you practice awhile, you start to develop confidence in what can strip negativity right off. "Use salt!" some workers say. Others, "just smudge that!" Those methods do work, but they're akin to having the word "password" for your password: people use them so often that anyone wanting to stop you from living

in peace is going to find a way to get around or through them. If a curse involves salt, countering it with salt does little or worsens the problem. They may also use anything from superglue to *garapata* (tick) extract to make their energy extremely difficult to remove. When someone has the motivation to harm you, they will find a way to do it.

Personal Effects

The most common method of casting a spell on someone involves using an item that belongs to that person, preferably their DNA. While blood, hair, and nail clippings are most common, they are far from the only option. A pen that you touched or a plant on your desk at work can act like a link because of the natural oils on your skin. Once, my friend and I both got hit by a nasty throat-closing spell from a jealous romantic rival. We realized that she gathered our napkins from a dinner we attended together. She wasn't sure which napkin belonged to which person, so she threw both into her spell. Everything that attacked me also attacked my friend! While we could recall our energy from that source, it took us a bit of time to even figure out how she had gotten anything. We knew when we were walking into a snake pit and did our best to clean up after ourselves, but we missed that one precious detail. You will usually miss something. And even if you don't, the level of attention to detail required to cover all your tracks would draw attention to yourself.

Minimize Garbage

The environmentally minded witch may encourage you to reduce, reuse, and recycle already, just out of kindness to the planet we share. But there's a more immediate reason to keep your garbage to a minimum: troublemakers. When someone wants your DNA, your garbage is the first place they look.

I was appalled to read a newsletter from a witch shop that included how to get at your cursing target. While accurate, it encouraged readers to violate most stalking laws. I am not against hexing in principle: in fact, I am of the philosophy that some people just need a good hexing. That said, abide by the law or principles of honor while doing so as much as possible. Someone may dig through your garbage. They may watch what you touch on your desk at work. They may take something from the bathroom stall right after you've used it. Some might even grab items you donate to a thrift store.

Footprints

A lot of us neglect our feet, and that includes forgetting to shield them. It's too easy to trip over something laid in our path. If you walk on grass (or snow), someone can scrape up the soil where you stepped, which is one way to cross you from your root to your crown. If someone doesn't know where you live, they can plant something next to the driver's side of your car, in the doorway of your workplace, or at the coffee shop where you most cross paths with others.

Your digital footprint can also trip you up. Old photos on social media are especially a problem, particularly since posting photos of yourself is practically demanded if you do anything remotely creative. There are many ways to minimize the damage, but the level of vigilance it takes may not be worth the effort. It's still a good idea to delete old social media accounts and take down old photos from time to time, rather than allowing a repository to build.

Spells to Recall Your Energy Signature

The previous passage almost definitely scared the daylights out of a few of you. Rather than wrapping yourself in plastic (please be sure to poke in some breathing holes!) and hiding in a back room for the rest of your life, you can take a few extra steps to ensure your relative safety from nefarious magicians. After all, if you're having a DNA-theft level of problem with another magickal person, you're likely somewhat prepared. This level of shenanigans very rarely happens to magical beginners.

Many spellcasters may tell you that once someone has your DNA, you're screwed. But the truth is that you're only screwed if you choose to believe you're screwed. You have two things working for you that most people fail to consider.

First, there's a biological statute of limitations on most of these spells. Every seven years, the cells on your body renew—you have completely different cells than you did seven years prior. That means that for most of these spells, unless someone refreshes at a disturbingly persistent rate, they simply stop applying to you. However, most of you do not have seven years to wait out a curse. Second, anything that truly belongs to you on an energetic level— and your body is incontrovertibly your own—can return to you.

You will need to use more than surface cleansing techniques to break a link. To be clear, you still need those methods—do *not* discard them. When you take a spiritual bath and smoke cleanse followed by proper cut and clear work, it makes the more stubborn energy areas easier to find. (Performing cut and clears is discussed in greater detail in chapter five.) These basic clearings make deeper attachments that hide in and on you more visible. This way, you can see and feel where your real work needs doing.

If someone has your DNA, you are more likely to experience sensations related to the area the DNA belonged to. Pains in the

feet and hands can indicate nail clippings. Pains in the head or dizziness, fuzziness, and cognitive issues usually means someone has
hair off your head. You can guess what happens if someone got
your pubic hair.

As said before, whatever belongs to you can be summoned
back to yourself. While some people might break a link, I prefer
to recall my energy because there's always a risk that the energy's
sender could renew your cord. With a recall, all that's left of the
stolen DNA is dead carbon.

YOU WILL NEED:

A jar with a lid

Some of your DNA—the gross stuff: hair, nail clippings,
blood, and so on—so we know what energy we're calling

A receptive lodestone, one that pulls rather than pushes to
draw your energy back to you, or a magnet

Copper wire (optional)

Any kind of white salt to take the energy conduction and
turn it back

Baking soda, a neutralizer of the initial spell

Water or your favorite beverage

Any small battery-operated LED light to act as a lure

I encourage you to burn incense or pray over each item while
telling it what you want it to do. This process helps you connect
to the energies of each object as you build a cohesive magickal
machine. In the jar, place your magnet and your DNA. If you
happen to have copper wire, wrap that around the magnet and
the gross stuff. Next, pour the salt so that it surrounds but does

not cover the magnet. Sprinkle about a tablespoon of baking soda on top. Add water or your favorite beverage. Seal the jar. Place the LED light on top, switch it on, and say, "I call myself back to myself. I set this light to guide my way."

In about twenty-four hours, you should feel less twitchy. Place this magickal machine somewhere only you know about. Shelving over refrigerators is great for this, as is the broiler drawer in older stoves.

It's important to know that cleansing is an inescapable practice for spiritual people. We must cleanse our bodies, our homes, and our spirits regularly. Between what gets sent deliberately and what we catch by accident, we always have something on us that needs to go.

Much of magick is just cleaning. The cleaning does teach us; as we scrub off the ick, we reveal ourselves and notice our changes. While perhaps cleaning up after a psychic attack serves as a negative motivator, the cleansing required forces us to build our skills.

FIVE

CHASE OFF THE SMALL STUFF

Daily Maintenance for Evil Eye, Gossip, and Other Annoyances

In the day-to-day of living as witches, we encounter a certain degree of ... stuff. The majority of stuff comes from strong feelings. Witchy folks are, collectively, an emotional lot. A common error magickal people make is attempting to make all of our intense and uncomfortable emotions go away instead of feeling and addressing them. As a result, we subconsciously and consciously send out good and bad energy all the time and sometimes do not take stock of the effect of what we are doing or its consequences when an emotion finally does get us to feel it. The better we practice physical, emotional, and spiritual cleansing, the less the cloud-o-stuff affects us, and the less we accidentally send out our bad vibes.

The following spells negate general bad vibes. Most of these jinxes and hexes do not happen because of a planned attack; they happen because someone doesn't regulate their own energy well. Consider these your baseline defenses after establishing a routine cleansing and self-care practice.

Evil Eye Protection

The evil eye, or *malocchio*, might sound less scary if we called it what it is: epic stink eye. Some people give a dirty look and repeat it often in the direction of those who inspire their disapproval or envy. The directed glare can lead to an energy buildup that manifests as a streak of bad luck. Evil eye drip rarely extends beyond normal bad-day stuff. Often enough, we also know it happened. For example, a woman once looked at my Nissan Leaf and commented, "Nice car," her voice dripping with scorn. I checked the energy on my car. Sure enough, she had evil-eyed my innocent and practical EV. In that case, all I needed to do was trace a pentagram in the air over the car and tell it to banish that gross stuff before I drove it again. The following methods should clear this particular type of metaphysical sliming.

Evil Eye Bath

Spiritual baths have a long and rich tradition. When we cleanse ourselves, we reset our energy. If you have reason to abstain from all exposure to alcohol, substitute a tea made from hops flowers and a pinch of yeast for the beer. As you run water in your bathtub, pour in:

One can or bottle of beer

1 C Epsom salts

½ T alum crystal

Some people practice a ritual bath where you kneel in the tub, pour the water over your head, and pray for about seven to nine minutes. I prefer to soak for twenty minutes. As you take this bath, pray to your divine source to clear off all jealousies, aspersions, and spite. Once finished bathing, put on a robe if you must, and let yourself air dry. The evaporation carries any additional lingering negativity off you.

Spell: Evil Eye House Protection
This doubles as a house warding method and general anti-jealousy protection. Print or draw this image on paper:

On the back, write:

> *Turn back the jealousy,*
> *Turn back the hate,*
> *Each finger delivers*
> *To the sender*
> *The intended fate.*

Anoint the eye with a drop or two of Evil Eye oil (recipe next). Stick the talisman to your window with double-sided tape. You can make one for each window.

SPEAK WORDS AGAINST THE EVIL EYE

Sometimes you just need to use your words. If you don't have time or space to make an oil or craft a charm, spoken spells make the perfect go-to. When you speak an incantation, breathe from your diaphragm and project the words. When you use a spoken spell to tell energy to get lost, it works far better if it sounds like you mean it!

When walking into a room that feels malignant, say:

> *Jealousy fall from here*
> *To earthing ground and rest*
> *That you may turn inward*
> *And see that you are blessed*
> *In the soil seed sunlight*
> *That you find true delight*

Recipe: Evil Eye Protection Oil

The most efficient way to seal yourself against influence is to anoint yourself with oils. They absorb into your skin and combine with your energy, adding a sort of weight to your etheric bodies. They also stay on much longer than waters or perfumes so you can potentially go through the entire day wearing only one application. Anoint the following spots: bottom of your feet, behind your knees, inside your elbows, the back of your neck, the middle of your forehead, the crown of your head, and both palms.

Plenty of purveyors of occult goods make their own Evil Eye oil. If you prefer to make your own, this recipe takes up to thirteen days to mature.

YOU WILL NEED:

2 mason jars with lid, plus a strainer

1 bulb garlic

2 T wormwood leaf

1 T mint, any type

1 T rosemary

1 T rue

⅛ T black walnut hull

Olive oil

For spray (optional):

Vodka

Distilled water

Spray bottle

Place all dry ingredients in a mason jar. Pour olive oil over the herb mixture until covered. Use a spoon or chopstick to press out any air bubbles. Top off the jar with oil, and close tightly. Shake once a day while repeating the spoken spell against jealousy. Do this for seven to thirteen days. At the end of this period, strain the oil into a new jar. Bury the remaining herbs on the edge of your property. Use this formula to anoint items around your house. Dilute a small amount of oil with vodka and distilled water to use as a general area spray.

Gossip Stoppers

In my experience, most psychic attacks begin with gossip. Someone speaks badly of their target, and the words stir others to dish about that person. Not too long after, the miasma dogpiles on the object of this gossip. Most often, the ones hurt worst by this attack were minding their own damn business. Fortunately, spells to still flapping tongues abound in almot every culture that has gossips.

Recipe: Stop Gossip Oil

Note: Do not let this oil contact your bare skin! The red pepper flakes will burn you. Wear gloves when mixing it, and use cotton swabs to apply it. To use, anoint charm bags, or effigies of stitched lips, and mark lines on doorways.

YOU WILL NEED:

1 mason jar with lid

1 T lavender buds, to calm minds

1 T alum crystal, to convulse tongues

½ t red pepper flakes, to burn the nastiness

1 to 2 C sunflower oil as carrier oil

Mix all dry herbs in a mason jar. Cover with sunflower oil. Use a chopstick or similar poking device to press out the bubbles, and then top off with the oil. Close lid tightly and store in a cool, dry place.

Once a day for seven days, shake the jar and speak this chant. Repeat it until you feel as though all energy possible has been released.

Bite your tongue, stop your bitter hate

Your evil only hits your pate

Speak against me—a callout awaits!

Tongues, Lips, and Gags: *Silencing the Spiteful*

Stop gossip, or *tapa boca*, as you may see printed on candles from botanicas, is one of the most straightforward-in-intent defensive spells. If you want to shut someone's mouth, you need something to represent a mouth or a tongue. The especially ambitious might add ears and eyes.

Sometimes, the indiscreet don't recognize your presence, and you end up hearing the gossip about yourself firsthand. When this happens, you don't need to run home or to your nearest botanica. You merely need to carry two lesser-known tools important to all magick workers: a notebook and a pen. The creative among us often have these handy. While an unlined notebook is ideal for most on-the-go workings, any notebook will work well. In the land of Solomonic workings, all blank paper counts as fresh parchment to the determined.

Sketch the mouth or head of the gossip. Write their name (if you know it) and any specific attributes such as their birthday, hair color, and eye color. Draw several tiny x marks over the mouth and write a directive that they do not speak of you across the lips.

If you wish to never deal with them again, sketch an x over each eye so that they won't see you or your doings. If you want to make sure they can't get dirt on you, add an x over the ears to prevent them from hearing about you.

Tuck the paper in a book no one reads or put it in a file drawer and forget it. If after a few months the gossip becomes irrelevant and you happen to come across the slip of paper, burn it and move on.

Spell: Stop Gossip Candle

There's a reason candle spells are popular: after dressing the candle, the flame does the rest of the work. Aside from cleanup, candle spells require little in the way of follow up.

I often recommend burning a stop gossip candle the moment you suspect any kind of attack. Getting others to talk poorly of you or even listen to negative words about you can have a cumulative negativity effect. It can lay the foundation for worse things to happen to your energy later.

YOU WILL NEED:

One seven-day glass-encased candle, white, blue, or purple

A barbecue skewer

A black marker

Any gossip stopper/*tapa boca*/STFU oil

One pinch of alum crystal powder

One pinch of lavender

One pinch of black pepper

One fire and rustproof bowl (for fire safety)

1 C water

Take the barbecue skewer and poke three holes in the candle. You may need to upend the candle and shake out the excess wax. Next, take the marker and write "stop gossip" and add any symbols that project "silence!" Add the names of anyone you know who speaks ill of you. Then carefully fill each hole with the Stop

Gossip oil and sprinkle one pinch of the alum, lavender, and black pepper on top of the candle. Place the candle in the bowl, pour the water around it, and light.

If you wish, add an incantation. In my case, I'm not very poetic. It usually goes, "All y'all, shut the hell up!"

Spell: Spiderweb Gossip Stopping

Oh, what a tangled web we weave whence we practice to deceive.
—Shakespeare, *A Midsummer Night's Dream*

Let's say some of those rumors about you have gotten especially … creative. Somehow you went from "I saw them having coffee" to starting an underground cult that collects wild turkeys and smuggles them into unsuspecting funeral homes. Now your turkey farmer boyfriend won't speak to you. Whatever the rumor, it's causing you problems.

This spiteful creativity is the mark of spider energy. Spiders weave, for good and bad. That's why spider spirits are considered the first storytellers. They can trap what you don't want, but that energy also leads to a lot of misinformation when wrong.

If you want to trap that bad news at its source, you can do this one of two ways: get a real spiderweb. (You can gather them with a little tissue from almost any corner of a slightly unkempt house or your yard, or anywhere. Spiders see structures and pretty much think, "let's build a web on this!") Or if arachnophobia paralyzes you, the second option is to make a web out of black construction paper. Look up directions for a kirigami spiderweb online. Remember, spiderwebs need are sticky, so swipe the paper with a glue stick before use.

YOU WILL NEED:

One whole lemon

A paring knife

Spiderweb, real or paper

A jar if you want this silencing to go on forever, a paper cup
if you want the working to disappear eventually

A napkin and a string if you opt for the paper cup

A slip of paper with the gossip's name

A pinch of alum crystal (to sour the tongue)

7 to 13 whole cloves (to compel silence)

A little bit of poppy seed (to make their words confusing and
irrational)

Make a single incision in the lemon, and stuff it with the name
paper and herbs. Wrap the spider webbing around the lemon. If
it's easier, stick the web over the incision to trap the herbs inside
the lemon. If you plan on making this spell long-term, place the
web encased lemon in your jar and seal it tight. Write a date on
the jar and your intention (but not the person's name). Put it in
a dark place. I have a "naughty shelf" in my garage that I clean
out once a year to store works against magickal miscreants. The
lemon will rot slowly over time, and the person will end up tangled in the very trouble their gossip would have otherwise caused.

If you want a temporary working, place the lemon in the
paper cup, cover it with a napkin and use the string to tie the
napkin over the top. Bury it or throw it in a dumpster, such as
the dumpster at a funeral home. If you choose to place it there,
make a water offering to the spirit of the place for their kindness

in allowing you to use their facilities. The lemon, cup, paper, and string will rot fast, and that gossip will disappear.

Spell Breaking

If you ran any diagnostics on yourself from the previous chapters and found a hex or spell, first try to break it. I keep a small set of "break in case of emergency" tools, usually a stack of herbs, oils, and ammonia powder.

Recipe: Spell Breaker Oil

Chant as you compose this recipe. The resulting oil can then serve as a spell-breaker spell all on its own or you can use it to anoint candles and effigies. You can also add a few drops to your bathwater or body wash as part of ritual cleansing.

YOU WILL NEED:
    Five drops of lavender
    One drop of camphor
    Three drops of benzoin
    Olive oil

Mix essential oils in a one-dram glass vial, and fill to the top with olive oil.

Spell Breaker Chant

You can speak this spell on its own or pair it with a ritual action. I use this myself while also pantomiming ritual "cuts" on myself with an obsidian knife. (I do not need to break the skin, as the knife only severs energetic rather than skin-based connections.) I chant as I cut energy cords off myself.

Say:

> *Gather spells against my person fragile and strong*
> *Smite them, stop them from carrying on*
> *Break every link, and the contract made*
> *Burn off the effect of tools of the trade*
> *Shut off portals and astral projection*
> *Shatter all magic on me that merits objection*

Repeat until you feel the negativity lift from you.

Protection Spells

Protection is one of the necessary day-to-day parts of practicing witchcraft. The world has a lot of spheres of influence floating through it. No matter how impressive, no mortal can track for every single intention or possibility they may encounter.

To make matters more complicated, magick from other people intended as positive may have undesired consequences or unknown circumstances that may require shielding. As an example, let's say you work a love attraction spell and someone responds. A rival you didn't know about catches wind of the working and works a spell to create obstacles for you and the person you desire. Or (if everyone has good intentions), they work a glamour to become more attractive to your intended and that glamour cancels out your own attraction work. When it happens, it feels like something invisible smacked you. You didn't experience a psychic attack, but you might receive it that way if you're new. In other situations, you might perform an uncrossing to remove one problem and find that another held out by the first block takes its place. My advice is always to have protection going, whether it's a candle burning, a charm carried in your pocket, or a daily prayer practice. Though the following spells and practices protect against deliberate action, accidental action can breed as much or more chaos as an intentional hex or curse. Daily cleansing and small protections can reduce magickal fender-benders.

Jewelry

A lot of witchy types love their protective jewelry, and for good reason. The shiny pretties do a lot of good stuff! Different metals can block specific energies, magnets can draw desired aid, and different stones can alter energy as you receive it. Choosing a metal that matches the shape of the symbol's intention can further refine your wards. Protective jewelry works best when in contact with your skin, and all the better where a casual passerby can't see it.

Charging Protection Jewelry

I like to work with a simple elemental altar dedicated to activating magickal objects. If you already work with elementals, you can likely skip the altar and simply direct the energy.

YOU WILL NEED:

Incense (any fragrance) and incense holder

A dish of salt

A tea light candle

A cup of water

Set up the altar with each element representation around a square. Western esoteric practices tend to assign the incense to the east, the candle to the south, the water to the west, and the salt to the north. Work with whatever arrangement speaks to you.

Light the incense, saying, "I invite the presence of the element of air."

Light the candle, saying, "I invite the presence of the element of fire."

Take a sip of the water, saying, "I invite the presence of the element of water."

Taste the salt, saying, "I invite the presence of the element of earth."

Hold the jewelry over the incense, then over the flame, then dunk it in the water, and then let it rest in the salt. At each one, state, "Imbue this with the most protective qualities of your element." You may want to imagine the element experiencing the jewelry or the jewelry experiencing the element to enhance this.

After you complete the elemental blessing, you can ask for the specific blessing of a deity you work with on an item. Hold the piece in your hand and pray to the power for a blessing of protection on the piece. Once you complete the prayer, it's ready to wear. You might want to repeat this ritual every six weeks; energetic charges wear down and sometimes need a boost.

Keep in mind that distinctive jewelry creates a tactical disadvantage: it gives a would-be attacker a way to connect to your energy and verify that it's you. Metals are conductive and can serve as energy beacons. If you like to wear protective amulets and talismans, change them from time to time.

Sigils

Sigils are popular for a reason: you can design any symbol, charge it with your intention using any energy source you like, and put it to work. While most people like a pen and paper to start drawing sigils, you can create them through visualization alone. You can also outsource the effort: several websites and phone apps offer sigil generators. The program designs it, you use your personal energy to charge it. For protection, sigils serve best when you know what you're dealing with. If, for instance, the intrusive energy you experience is from a general emotional outburst and not from designed intention, you will need to adapt the sigil accordingly. Banishing external energy is very different from banishing someone's emotional state, especially if they're dwelling on you and thus creating even more of a charge to what they send.

Cosmetics

Makeup has a long history as a tool of ritual transformation. We use it to either hide or reveal ourselves, depending on what we wish to express. Cosmetics give us a potent tool and opportunity, one that we can buy at the corner drugstore! Eyeliner, for example, protects from the evil eye. While drawing attention, red lipstick also creates a defense so that others cannot turn your words back on you. Writing or sketching symbols on yourself can go a long way toward adding that extra bit of safety and defense. If you prefer to keep your cosmetics covert, you can charge and bless lip balms, skin lotions, and even clear mascaras.

Witch Bottles

A witch bottle is a jar filled with urine, broken glass, pins, rusty razors and nails, and other DNA pieces. The gross and very useful witch bottle spell has existed so long that archaeologists still find buried bottles of ick in building foundations. They also continue to act surprised by this, despite a news report about someone finding one surfacing roughly one to two times a year. Most people seeking magickal protection only ever need to make a witch bottle once. Continuous protection involves something with more commitment and less disgusting material.

The purpose of the bottle is to create a decoy. Carefully fill a bottle with the stuff described above and add a slip of paper with "Over here, stupid!" or a similar taunt written in red or black ink. Attackers that might have your DNA will float over there, then the sharp things in the bottle stick them. I suggest making one once a year as a precaution. And if you don't like the idea of peeing in a bottle, you can substitute liquid ammonia or apple cider vinegar.

Spell: Protection Jar

The protection jar spell does something a little different from a witch bottle. A protection jar, unlike a witch bottle, is magick you work continuously. The jar creates a layer of containment to your energy, acting as a protection shield so that you no longer have to tire yourself out maintaining a visualization of a shield around your person.

YOU WILL NEED:

One mason jar, any size, with a lid

A photo of yourself and any household members you wish to protect. If a photo isn't possible, write out full names on a slip of paper.

A photo of your home, if possible

Honey

Cloves

Cinnamon

Mint, any type

Sewing pins

Red wine or grape juice

Tea light candle

Frankincense essential oil and iron powder (both optional)

Place the photos at the bottom of the jar facing up. Cover them with honey. Add the herbs so that they completely cover the photos. Add a layer of sewing pins. Pour red wine or grape juice over all of it, calling to the herbs and pins for robust protection as you do. Close the jar tight. Place this in a high traffic part of your home. For most people, the kitchen stove is fine, but fireplaces also work. Once a week (more if needed), burn a tea light on top of it and pray for surrounding protection.

Spell: Sleep Protection Incantation

Speak this incantation before you sleep. You need no other tools beyond your imagination.

> *Power of earth guard my slumber*
>
> *Water pulls all troubling aims under*
>
> *Fire changes dark dreams to nighttime wonder*
>
> *Air misdirect evil sent my way*
>
> *Spirit preserve me from the nighttime fray*

Spell: Candle Protection

If you need to raise energy immediately but don't have a lot of time to spare, light a candle colored red, white, or purple. Each color has a high enough frequency to generate much-needed power in a pinch. Focus on the flame and repeat this chant for seven minutes. Yes, it's okay to set a timer to make sure you hit that exact amount of time.

Chant:

> *Enfold me*
>
> *Surround me*
>
> *Above and below*
>
> *Lay what would harm me*
>
> *Far*
>
> *Wide*
>
> *And low*

House Protection Spells

When energies get thrown at both person and home, it's often tempting to put the needs of home first. We're wired for that; we see our shelters as extensions of ourselves. The proper order, however, should always be yourself first and then your home. After all, if you're dirty and decide to clean the house, you're going to track dirt everywhere. Once you bathe and add that protection oil, roll up your sleeves and start on your dwelling. Plan on taking a second shower when you're done.

Spell: Elemental Protection

Many people think of their home as something that stands between them and the forces of nature. To some extent, that's true: a roof keeps precipitation off your head, the walls keep uninvited critters from crawling into bed with you, and doors and windows signify a division between you and the rest of the world. But that protection only lasts until such a time that nature decides to remind you that She Always Wins. You can reduce if not negate the impact of the forces of nature upon your home by befriending the elements. Having this relationship adds another layer of protection, as elemental entities can neutralize many commonplace curses.

Note: I encourage those who can do so to circumambulate their home for each element. If you can't do this, imagine a projection of yourself floating through your home doing the same thing.

Begin at the center of your living space. If the layout has no clear center, stand where you cook. The hearth carries the energy of the house center, even if architects don't design around them anymore.

Face each cardinal direction and invite the element and its spirits to be a part of your household. Walk through every room in your house, repeating this invitation for each element.

Repeat this process for each room of your home, repeating the invitation to the elements. When finished, return to your stove.

FACING EAST
"Powers of the east, elements, and elementals of air and wind, speech and communication—that which fills our lungs and clears our minds—I call you out from the nooks and crannies, the space between spaces of this home and ask that you join us as household members. As part of this household, I ask that you protect us from all forces sent from your domain and that you do all you can to keep us in a spirit of cooperation with the kingdom of the air. Be part of our home. Come, be part of the family! Let Archangel Raphael and King Paralda guide your way!"

FACING SOUTH

"Powers of the south, elements, and elementals of fire and heat, transformation and destruction—that which animates us and calls us to magick—I call you out from the nooks and crannies, the space between spaces of this home and ask that you join us as household members. As part of this household, I ask that you protect us from all forces sent from your domain and that you do all you can to keep us in a spirit of cooperation with the kingdom of fire. Come, be part of the household. Come, be part of the family! Let Archangel Michael and King Djinn guide your way!"

FACING WEST

"Powers of the west, elements, and elementals of water and moisture, emotion and flow—that which fills our blood and loosens our bodies—I call you out from the nooks and crannies, the space between spaces of this home and ask that you join us as household members. As part of this household, I ask that you protect us from all forces sent from your domain and do all you can to keep us in a spirit of cooperation with the kingdom of water. Come, be part of the household. Come, be part of the family! Let Archangel Gabriel and King Necksa guide your way!"

FACING NORTH

"Powers of the north, elements, and elementals of earth and soil, stability and foundation—that which builds our bones and pulls us to the roots—I call you out from the nooks and crannies, the space between spaces of this home and ask that you join us as household members. As part of this household, I ask that you protect us from all forces sent from your domain and do all you can to keep us in a spirit of cooperation with that of the kingdom of earth. Come, be part of the household. Come, be part of the family! Let Archangel Uriel and King Ghob guide your way!"

You may wish to repeat the above working at each season. If you live in a place where seasons are subtle and strange, set your personal calendar according to the behavior of the environment. You can build an altar or simply do a little tea tray of offerings every so often to let the elements and elementals know you appreciate everything they do for you and your household.

GENERAL WARDING METHODS

Warding is what it sounds like: a way of keeping things out. Most people that set wards use them as passive workings, usually as metaphysical walls of resistance. For most people, this works fine, much like locking your doors and windows. However, when someone is determined to attack, they may attack your defenses before they even consider attacking you, just as a determined burglar will smash in the windows or destroy security cameras. Passive wards, effectively energetic "keep out" signs, are the easiest to knock out.

Some of us, however, live in the energetic version of bad neighborhoods. That will typically require a little more security than a lock or a wall. What I recommend is layering wards, mixing the passive and active. You best know your situation and what warding you will genuinely need.

Use this list of warding types to help design your defenses.

Offensive: If triggered, this ward attacks the attacker

Reflective: Sends energy back

Absorptive: It catches and stores the sent energy; this works best with an added layer that cleanses or converts that energy

Traps: Ensnares the energy/sendings for you to release or destroy later

Destructive: Burns, drowns, explodes, or otherwise obliterates sendings (and sometimes the sender). It is not an attack because it only responds when triggered and does not chase down the sender; it works when the sender approaches you and your space.

Swallows: This literally takes everything and throws it down a portal, not to resurface until the next supernova.

Sentient: Wards as guards empowered with decision-making abilities; this is usually either hired spirits or constructed servitors

Passive: Keep things out

Most people are fine with one or two ward types. However, a few of us must put time and effort into layering our options if we ever want to engage in otherwise normal activities like sleeping peacefully.

DOORS AND WINDOWS

Always ward points of entry first. Doors and windows are inherently liminal spaces. Because they form thresholds between your home and outside your home, energies and beings can linger in that space. Even in the world where all is just energy, people still need to pass through those doors and windows to get into your house. Ward well, but accept that crossing entries always demands some degree of vulnerability.

Simple pieces of home décor also serve as talismans of protection. For instance, cinnamon brooms hung above doors and windows sweep off the negative energy of those passing beneath, adding a little bit of burning fire to the removal of trouble. If you prefer more subtlety than a broom, you can bless and charge already present curtains, blinds, or wall hangings. Pray over or concentrate on the fabric with your intention until it feels different in your hands. Once you feel the change, tell it what you want it to do to protect your home.

DOOR PROTECTIONS—WREATHS

When crafted with intent, a wreath can serve as a ward, spirit portal, and sometimes even a trap. Wreaths also make lovely, unremarkable home decorations—few people think anything of a front door with a wreath on it.

For home protection, I suggest two types of wreaths. One is passive, to act as an energetic "stop." Think of it as a large-chested giant that stuff just bounces off. The other wreath is active; it consumes and then converts energy. What it consumes then gets "excreted" and stored within the items you hang on the wreath. That energy can continuously power your house protections.

You can purchase a pre-woven unadorned wreath from any craft store or make your own. I prefer to buy a plain one and put the rest of my time into the items that decorate it.

Passive Protection Wreath

This wreath serves as a sort of nightclub bouncer that reacts to what comes through your door with passive resistance.

YOU WILL NEED:

Small squares of white paper

A pen or sharpie

One red and one yellow ribbon

A glue gun

Scissors

Fresh herbs still on the stems, such as lavender, rue, and rosemary

Any charms, symbols, or pictures you wish to add

On the paper, write down who and what has permission to enter your home. Think of this as the security checklist for your house. You might say "my ancestors" or specific names of deities you worship. If relevant, add members of your household and their known protector spirits. Include your pets. Wrap these into small scrolls and tie the ribbon. Hold each scroll in your hand, visualizing it as a small key.

Set the scrolls aside—they're the fussiest bit, so they go into the wreath last. Weave in the herbs, spreading them out so that they form a complete circle. Talk to the herbs about the protections and how you want them to keep out disease(s). You can look up the folkloric applications of herbs in such references as *Cunningham's Encyclopedia of Magickal Herbs* and gear your words to the plants' known associations.

Tuck the scrolls around the wreath, distributing them as evenly as possible. Last, glue on the charms and pictures. If it feels right, add images of deities, saints, protection symbols, and locks and keys. Use whatever speaks to your heart and hearth. As you do this work, think about what you want each piece of the wreath to do and how you want to see them perform together.

When completed, take a moment to lay your hands on the wreath and connect to its energy. See it strengthening your home, standing firm against all intrusion. Lovingly hang it on your door. Reinforce it by anointing it with a protection oil once a week and changing the wreath's herbs every month.

Active Protection Wreath

This wreath doesn't just resist intrusion—it takes an active role in protecting your home by grabbing the energy and ... well, eating it.

YOU WILL NEED:

Pins—slide-in jewelry pins are ideal, but standard sewing pins can work

Nails made from an alloy that includes iron

Yarn—dark blue, black, and purple

A glue gun

Any black stone—tourmaline is ideal

While the making of the wreath is more straightforward than the previous one, it is more complicated magic. Expect to spend a little more time with this project than the material list might suggest.

Insert the pins and nails evenly around the wreath, spacing them as evenly apart around the wreath as you can manage. Imagine each one as a defensive sword that can slice to bits any attack energy. Place the wreath facedown. Take the black yarn and weave it to cross the center of the wreath from several angles. Repeat this with the blue thread. The crossing of the threads forms a spirit trap. Weave half the purple yarn counterclockwise around the wreath, wrapping it in a spiral around the form's edge. Purple in this context is a color of domination: it will overpower and consume sent spirits or shut them out as the intelligence you imbue in the wreath deems appropriate. Glue the stone on the back of the wreath near the bottom, at a point that intersects with the threads. The tourmaline acts as the storage battery to contain what the threads might capture.

Spend time concentrating on each part of the wreath. The black strings are to catch things invisible to you, while the blue entangles more obvious sendings. The purple overpowers anything sent. Focusing on the inner circle, the wreath's blank space, imagine it as a doorway to a black hole. If anything gets past the trap, it gets sucked in.

Take your time working with the energy on this. Once you get it working, it pays off as a self-sustaining protection system.

DOORWAYS

Doorways and door frames can call for tough protection measures. Because entrances serve as in-between spaces, spirits and people with skill at liminal works and threshold magic may well break through them or simply plant trouble right in that between space. A belief that evil spirits haunt thresholds goes back to the times of the ancient Greeks and Romans. Even back then, a groom lifted the bride over the doorway lest spirits attach through the soles of her feet!

Over-the-door charms have long traditions behind them. Choose one as befits your heritage and inclinations. But you can go further. While horseshoe and broom charms excel at keeping out evil and brushing away negative vibrations, a few enhancement tools such as anointing oils can help for those hopefully rare occasions when someone attempts to take a battering ram to your defenses.

PROTECTIVE OILS AND POWDERS

Lining your doorways with cascarilla (chalk made from eggshell) limits what can cross to either side. The disadvantage is that you need to refresh the chalk line daily if you use your door. You can also anoint doorways with a protection oil of your choice; a little goes a long way. Other protections can include hanging crossed nails and other items with iron in them, as well as sprinkling a teaspoon of brick dust across your doorways, as bricks have long been associated with fortified walls.

DOORMAT SPELLS

To stop trouble before it crosses your threshold, put a few drops of a defensive potion under your doormat. Renew this treatment every few days. You might also want to sketch a few symbols or words of protection in cascarilla under the mat. Establish clear rules about who may enter and who may not, and speak them aloud. Each time you repeat this spell, reinforce the rules for your household. You can do this in sigils and symbols, but I also recommend using your words: the more clearly you speak, the better your boundaries.

CORNERS AND SHADOWS

Every household has corners and shadowy areas where troubled energies can settle. Crumbling camphor chips in the corners of your room can clear out a lot of negativity. Additionally, I set jars of white vinegar and sea salt in these spots to neutralize negativity generated from bad moods or circumstances. If you feel you need more direct protection, you can hang or sketch protective symbols in the shadows or install LED strip lights to illuminate them. Reinforce with blessed water or protection oils weekly.

Trapping Small Spirits

Minor spirits can accidentally enter your home, but unless they are fae, either someone sent them or the spirits specifically want your attention. Sometimes a spirit in your house was summoned but never banished, and is now just hanging out. The worst problems happen when imps get loose. Imps are demonic pets (not demons) that are far more annoying than any demon. While spiteful, most are not smart. Many years ago, one of the other magician types in the shop I worked at once neglected to banish an imp after doing whatever it was they were trying to do. It kept harassing employees at the shop until a coworker used some biblical hoodoo on the damned thing. This situation inspired me to find another way to deal with the little bastards. If I had this tool available to me at the time, I would have used it. It would have saved me considerable annoyance. In retrospect, I should have demanded ransom from the demon pet-owner.

Working: Lesser Spirit Trap

When this works, you end up with a jar that feels oddly heavy given the small piece of chocolate and burnt candle. Often when I catch these, I give them to a demon companion who returns them to their owners with an admonishment to keep a closer eye on their imps.

YOU WILL NEED:

One jar with a lid

A glue stick

A printout or drawing of the seals—the Fifth Pentacle of Mars goes inside the jar lid. The Grand Pentacle goes underneath the jar, facing upwards.

A white Shabbat candle

Your hair, blood, nail clippings, whatever—only a little

A lighter, preferably a long one

Candy/chocolate

Rose thorns, spider webbing/cotton batting (both optional)

Glue the Fifth Pentacle of Mars on the inside of the jar lid and the Grand Pentacle on the bottom of the jar so that you can see it when you look inside the jar. Place the lid underneath the jar. Melt the candle a little bit on the bottom so that it stands up in the jar. Add your DNA, candy, and any of the thorns/trapping items you wish. Place the jar in the room of the activity and light the candle.

If you must leave the room, for the sake of safety, set the candle inside a much larger fireproof bowl. Set a timer. In most cases, these candles burn down in about thirty minutes, and you want to pay attention to the jar when the candle has about one inch of wax left. Once burned down to a stub, take the lid from under the jar and screw it closed. The lid will snuff the candle.

The jar will likely feel heavier than it did before you set the trap. That's how you know you trapped a spirit. You can bury the spirit, attempt to talk with it about where it came from, or release it far away from your home. If a spirit seems especially ill-tempered, I dispose of them in church or cemetery dumpsters, but only after making an offering to the place's spirit as a thank you.

Quick and Dirty Spirit Trap

If you don't want to mess around with candles and jars, you can trap a spirit with an empty wine bottle, a piece of chocolate, a bowl of water, and a little bit of your hair. Place the bowl of water in the room that has the most spirit activity. Set the wine bottle upright in the bowl and remove the cap or cork. Drop in the piece of chocolate and a bit of your hair. If you have a small enough LED light, drop a light set to "on" inside the bottle as well. Wait for four hours, and then recap the bottle. If it caught the spirit, it should feel heavier than when you started.

Uncrossing

Uncrossing works are a mainstay of both traditional British witch-craft and Southern Uniteed States folk magick. These workings remove spiritual debris from your path, including spells, curses, crossings, and, sometimes, the inner obstacles we create for ourselves. Some practitioners recommend performing an uncrossing at least once a month paired with a protection spell. It's also a good idea to perform one right before any goal-centered spell. For example, if you want to work money magick, using an uncrossing candle would remove the obstacles on the path to your objective.

Working: Simple Uncrossing

The following working is a fast uncrossing that requires few tools. I usually keep the materials for this on my working altar to clear a path before routine castings.

YOU WILL NEED:
Paper

Pen

Uncrossing oil

A match

A fireproof container

Write your name on a slip of paper. Take a little uncrossing oil and draw the sigil for the planet Saturn (shown above) over your name. Then burn the paper in the container while chanting until reduced to ash:

> *I break the cross*
> *I burn the hex*
> *I end all evil*
> *I am blessed*

You can compost the ashes or scatter them at a crossroads.

Working: Water-Based Uncrossing

If you can't burn things, use this uncrossing. For this, you only need a bath bomb (preferably lemon-scented) and a glass of water. I used to make "uncrossing bombs" for energy clearing before starting any kind of spellwork and still sometimes keep a few on hand. If you want to customize yours, you can find plenty of bath bomb recipes on the internet. They're a lot of fun to make!

Drop the bath bomb in a clear glass and perform a slightly modified chant:

> *I break the cross*
> *I melt the hex*

Evil dissolves
I am blessed

The dramatic fizz in the water can be extremely gratifying.

Working: Planetary Uncrossing

Sometimes, when your situation is especially tough, you need to level up your uncrossing methods. Most of what I do addresses earth-based energies. Some people use the planets in their workings, which means you need those planets represented in said workings. There are also people out there who are star-and-planet crossed. While it may take far more work than a simple uncrossing to address, the following working offers a place to start.

YOU WILL NEED:

A slip of paper for each planet you want to include

A marker

Any oils you want to anoint the papers with (uncrossing oil is used in the spell)

A fireproof container

Matches or a lighter

Water plus one other way to extinguish the fire if necessary

On each sheet of paper, write down the glyph for a different planet. Anoint with uncrossing oil. Burn the respective glyph as you say each line. Wait for each glyph to burn completely before moving on to the next paper.

Sun, remove your troubles sent to this place
Moon, recall demons sent and bind them out in space

Mercury, turn evils back to your plane

Venus, banish jealousies bane and vain

Mars, defeat sources of strife and aggression

Jupiter, consume what leads to oppression

Saturn, take back punishments and cruel tests

Uranus, gather all meant to obsess

Neptune, wash away chaotic mental sway

Pluto, take stolen spirits back to rest

Eris, gather your toys trouble the troublemakers next

Uncross this person, place, and time

Sink evil sent in primordial acid slime

Free them from all trouble sent

And when senders call for me, they can get bent.

Working: Cut and Clear

When a connection ends acrimoniously, it leaves those involved exposed to negative emotional energy from one another. Unless dealt with promptly, the negativity often escalates.

A cut and clear severs your energy from another person. This practice, also called clearing, comes in handy after any relationship ending. Depending on the nature of the relationship, this clearing may need more advanced techniques.

YOU WILL NEED:

Thread

Scissors

At least one lemon

OPTIONAL:

Cut and Clear or Blessing oil

Yellow candle

Licorice root

A bowl of water (if you opt for the candle)

The spell works well just with the lemon and string. Add fire energy if you want extra insurance that you burned off any loose ends/connections. Should you choose the candle, set up a ritual space that allows for fire containment. I like to do this on metal trays, but use whatever feels safe and works for you. Your space should have one glass candle, a bowl of water for the candle to sit in (fire safety), scissors, and thread.

TO PERFORM THE RITUAL:

Cut a piece of thread about the length of your arm.

Hold the thread between your hands and feel the connection between you and the other person. It's okay if some good memories pop up; good and bad tend to go together even in relationships that need to end. When you feel the energy building that tells you of the pull between you, tie the thread around either wrist. Pull the string taut and say:

> *The tie that binds*
> *Has pulled too tight*
> *[Name] and I are no longer right.*
> *With a snip and a snap, it falls away*
> *We've no more connection*
> *And no more to say!*
> *As I will, so mote it be!*

Cut the string where it circles your wrist. Wrap it around the outside of the candle. Next, cut the lemon in half to represent severance and cleansing. Light the candle. You can choose to let it burn down all the way, or you can let it burn for an hour a day until it burns down. Once the candle has burned down, dispose of the string in running water (whether toilet or river), or burn it. You can throw the rest of the spell in the garbage.

Banishing

While some magickal schools of thought advocate banishment as the best way to dismiss negative energy, it has limits. First, most people know about banishing and usually prepare to either boomerang what they sent back to you or have more to send. Second, this practice assumes a magickal construct comprises only one energy type, such as fire, when quality constructs use multiple elements and sources.

Also, a common issue with banishing: no one knows where something goes beyond "away." If you don't know where it went, you always risk it coming back.

Spell: Negativity Banishing for Love

Large swaths of negative energy invading your life can, over time, affect and ruin your closest relationships. If the people in your life mean something to you, it is important to keep those connections strong. Sometimes this requires a little rescue magick.

The following chant can act as a spell on its own. Speak it while burning incense or a candle for increased effect. While most people might use this after a fight with a loved one, it works well as a preventative.

Chant:

Behind me, the gate
Of bitterness and hate
Closes forever
the dam of joy breaks
Flooding me in love and true friendship
Filling my dance card, filling my plate
In loyalty, honor,
Goodwill and truth

Recipe: Banishing Incense

If you want an incense to burn as you perform a banishing chant, try this recipe. Add rose leaves (known for healing a broken heart) or substitute honey to alter it for banishing relationship damage.

YOU WILL NEED:

2 T molasses

¼ t asafoetida

1 t cinnamon

A pinch of chili pepper

1 t turmeric

1 t allspice

While mixing, chant:

Banish blight
Kill spot
By these herbs' power
Dissolve the knot!

Burn on charcoal incense. Warning: this smells terrible. Only burn it with open windows while using a fan.

Recipe: Banishing Oil
Use this on candles or dabbed on doorway thresholds and under welcome mats to turn back anything that might cause trouble.

YOU WILL NEED:

Per one-dram vial, add:

One drop of lilac fragrance oil*

Three drops of myrrh

Sweet almond oil, to top off vial

*You can use lilac petals instead, but the fragrance does not transfer as well. In this case, the synthetic usually matches the energy of the real lilacs.

Spell: To Banish an Annoying Human
This spell does not make someone disappear in a puff of smoke, but it does have a way of making someone suddenly extremely interested in being somewhere else.

YOU WILL NEED:

A piece of paper

A marker

A black or purple candle

A white candle

Write the name of the problematic person on a piece of paper. Place it under the black or purple candle dressed in banishing oil and light the candle.

For seven minutes, chant:

Be gone and take your obnoxious actions with you!

Light the candle daily until completely melted. Bury the remaining wax and paper away from your property. Wherever you dispose of it, bring an offering for the spirits of that space.

Once buried, go home, and light a white candle for seven minutes a day until it melts completely. During each burn, chant:

Bring in healthy folks, thoughts, and deeds.

When you first sense trouble, try the spells up to this point first. If the trouble runs deeper, then delve into the rest of the book.

The spells in this chapter serve as a baseline protection practice. If they seem like a lot of work, that's because they are! Those who work with spiritual forces must cleanse and ward all the time as a price for working with magic. For most people, the spells here will stem any onslaught of nonsense. The next chapters deal with deeper issues and require more care—especially self-care—to perform.

SIX

YOU DID *WHAT* NOW?
Bindings, Freezing, and Reversals
for Crossed Boundaries

Ugliness is part of human nature. Every time we develop
new tools, weapons, and skills, we gain an opportunity
to see this ugliness as a response to the beauty of creativity. Some people get jealous, cut down or downplay
accomplishments, or try to destroy the good they see so
that they feel no need to live up to the good in the world.
The solution to this pollution of human nature is deep
spiritual work. Sincere practitioners examine and heal
traumas and then strive for healthy boundaries. Once
in a while, one of those buttholes already has occult skill
and practice to apply to you.

North American–based folk magick uses four
primary methods of "knock it off" spells: binding,
freezing, reversing, and revoking. Each version of
"get off my lawn" takes a different approach to intrusive energy. In some situations, depending on the

persistence of the person sending, you may end up needing to use all methods. Much of the time, however, you will only need to use one. The trick with this entire class of spells is to do the work and forget about the people who prompted you to do it. After working one of these spells, reclaim that headspace someone rented for yourself. Bake some cookies, write a blog post, clean your house. Move forward.

Figuring Out What Happened

In order to counter a spell on yourself, you need to find out as much as you can about the magick used. General cleansings can get a lot of negative energies off you, deliberate or otherwise. However, people with real intention and practice can find ways to make spells "stick" to you, such as using garapata extract (made from ticks), soaking your name in molasses, or using hooks instead of pins in a poppet of you. To remove spells with that much planning and intention, it helps to know at least in general what type of spell someone used on you.

I focus here on the tarot as a way of identifying the specifics of a negative spell used. There are many other ways to get this information, some more advanced than others. If you have a relationship established with it, using a spirit board to communicate with a spirit ally can get you the details of the spell and sometimes even your assailant's name. Spirit evocation, in general, may or may not get you the information you want. Spirits get cranky when you cold-call them for an interrogation. They respond far better to offerings, good manners, and old fashioned hospitality—complete with good boundaries. Sometimes the spirit hired to harass you may communicate and even feel inclined to renegotiate its contract if offered hospitality. Other methods besides cards and a chat with a spirit exist in traditions beyond mine, and some folklore about those spirits may even tell you the kind of curses that lie on you.

Tarot is my preference because I have worked with its imagery for more than twenty years. The images, when read with a cursing context in mind, line up with spells I consider common. Any deck that resonates with you works fine for energy diagnostics. I prefer to use the Waite-Smith and Tarot of the Spirit by Pamela Eakins together. The Waite-Smith illustrates traditional witchcraft approaches well to my perception—it's easy to see bindings, cord cuttings, and isolations. Tarot of the Spirit takes a more astrologically focused worldview that allows a broader picture of blocked roads, cognitive traps, and how energy affects the inner and outer worlds. Between the two decks, I can see not only where bad energies lie but also the methods used for cursing.

The OK, Something Is Up, What Did They Do? Layout

Draw the first card to represent the querent. For this reading style, skip indicator cards (such as "tall, brown-eyed man is King of Wands"). The deck itself tells you either the role or the perception of the querent in this situation. The way any curse-sender sees the target can help you figure out what to do to clean it up, and sometimes who needs their energies muted.

Place the next four cards around the querent. These represent forces that surround this person. If the meaning seems murky, draw an additional two cards per "X" card for clarification. If the spread continues to lack clarity, someone may be using invisibility or confusion work, or a curse is not the problem. We will address ways to circumvent invisibility blocks in chapter seven.

The layout will look like this:

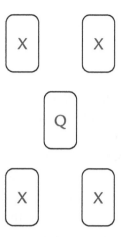

Certain cards are more likely than others to appear if intentional negative energy is afoot. This list is not exhaustive, nor do any of the cards mean that the energy originates in a curse. The meaning of tarot cards shifts based on the context of the cards that surround them, the reader, and the client's cultural context. For example, the Fool card usually indicates a curse is not the problem. However, it can also suggest that someone has the querent "fooled." If the client works as a stand-up comic, the Fool refers to their job and may indicate people they work with have issues, and so on.

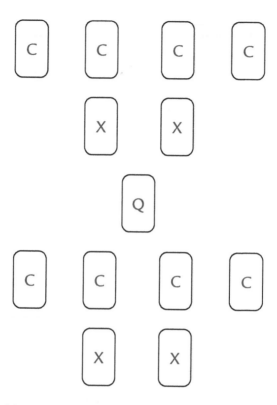

Tarot Cards of Cursing: Minor Arcana

The minor arcana shows us the petty details. And in the case of cursing, those details may be especially petty. Swords and wands are often indicators of conflict, while cups and pentacles signify motivations. However, the minor arcana gives no hints as to the intensity of the curse; most of the time, it shows the nuts and bolts of the personal situation and the underlying reasons. If you want to know the order of magnitude of a potential curse, use dice or playing cards. The lower numbers indicate less of an issue, the higher numbers indicate greater cause for concern.

Arcana	Common Element	Emotional Indicator	Motivation Indicator
Swords	Air	Cold anger, revenge, planned period efforts	Strategic: Calculation of violence, demonstration of dominance
Wands	Fire	Hot anger, passion, determination, persistence	Nonstrategic: Frustrated passion, entitlement
Pentacles	Earth	Greed, hunger, lust	Strategic: Seeking a specific end, recovering lost status (usually perceived)
Cups	Water	Grief, anguish, tears shed	Nonstrategic: Overwhelming passion, excessive pain

The Court Cards

Court cards, when mastered, can give personality descriptions of the spellcasters or spirits involved. In most cases, it is easy enough to figure out who cast a curse, sometimes even why, by recognizing the personality type. While court cards may not lead directly to any culprit, they give insight into the personalities at play in the querent's life and how those personalities mesh with their spiritual health.

Rather than list all the court cards and their traits, refer to each suit's essential traits. Assume that the ranking of page/knight, princess, queen, and king (or however your deck aligns them) indicates age *or* degree of power/control. Most of the time, this means that high ranking cards suggest a greater age, but these indicators shift based on the social context. The querent's boss might be ten years younger than them, but since that boss holds power over the querent, you may see a king instead of a knight.

Swords (Air)

Swords are the cards of strategy. While the sword's most common associated element of air is often considered intellectual and devoid of emotion, a lot of emotion must happen for swords to appear. Because swords are action cards like wands, they can reveal the type of spell used on someone. When it comes to identifying negative energies, know that the swords are not the rulers but the servants. They show actions taken because of the emotions, and no matter how well planned those actions, either the fire of anger or the water of grief brought the swords into the picture.

Two of Swords

In a cursing context, this card is an indicator of either invisibility or blinding work. It often suggests someone has gone to great pains to stay hidden. It can also suggest their tactics are mainly psychological, such as making the querent feel stuck between two bad choices. Only by removing the blindfold/glamour can the targeted person truly see no danger to letting go. It may also help them spot the opportunity that someone else wants them to miss.

Three of Swords

When this card shows up, someone wants you to see some suffering. The stabbed heart card frequently appears when someone has used effigy magick on the querent. It may also appear in social engineering trickery, such as when one person becomes the scapegoat of a social group.

Seven of Swords

While less evident in the Waite-Smith deck, the Tarot of the Spirit version of this card shows a pit of snakes, laying bare gossip and betrayal surrounding the querent. Within tarot symbolism, snakes frequently represent gossip, deception, and poisoning. Nearly all low-grade psychic attacks begin with gossip. People who engage in negative work can seldom keep themselves from talking about their exploits. Also, clever manipulators raise negative energy via a good old-fashioned session of badmouthing. Such methods can save a vengeful energy worker the expense of digging into their resources by raising others' ire and angry energy already directed at the target.

Eight of Swords
If the Eight of Swords shows up, someone likely performed a binding. Bindings can be tricky both to perform and experience. They impose limitations that, while annoying, can serve as protection. Think of the fairy tales where something terrible happens to the princess on her sixteenth birthday. Sure, something terrible happens *then*, but the conditions of the curse make her virtually immortal until that date. Many bindings are not malicious—high-handed, yes, but not malicious. Sometimes it's like a cosmic hug from a bossy parent.

Wands (Fire)
While we often look to the swords for overt violence, the fuel that feeds abusive cycles lives in the wands. These cards illustrate passions and extremes. All too often, a wand card reveals people controlled by their anger and struggling with choices made in moments of passion.

Ace of Wands, Direct
The Ace of Wands indicates the gathering of force. If it shows up when hex-detecting, a direct aspect suggests that someone is gathering their energy. Think of Ace of Wands as the microcosm

of the Magician; if the magician gathers energy and plans, the Ace of Wands grabs energy and improvises. If both cards appear in a spread, examine the cards that surround them to glean the context. It can indicate more than one person taking adverse action, a graduated plan (so a spell/hex repeats and replenishes fuel over time), or just that someone made plans involving you, possibly without your consent.

Five of Wands, Direct or Inverted

When reading for curses, the Five of Wands indicates an attack launched that either you or your spirits must fight off. If this card shows up in direct aspect, you likely already know you're in the thick of it. However, if it appears inverted, someone has taken steps to convince you that the daily aggressions are mere coincidence.

Seven of Wands, Direct

The Seven of Wands indicates a stream of continuous energy without well-shaped intention. This card appears most often for me in situations where land spirits and fae have taken offense at my choices. This card falling can also indicate a person with emotions so powerful that their feelings can take on a life of their own and function as spirits. For animists, this phenomena is subtly different from when the animistic spirits of emotions visit.

Ten of Wands, Direct

Should the Ten of Wands appear, you need to look as far under the layers of what's happening as you can because it seems that someone is trying to distract you from the true trouble source. Often the distraction happens in the form of too many things happening all at once.

Cups (Water)

The element of water contains the ebb and flow of emotions, whereas the wands sometimes represent the emotions themselves. When water appears in a cursing examination spread, someone lost equilibrium. Cups show deep motivations and sometimes complicating mental health factors. Often, it's here that we can identify the emotional signatures of our attackers. Because water flows until it finds a container, we can also reverse or divert these energies once we recognize them. Tarot does not ever diagnose someone's neurological state, but it can indicate where thought patterns and reasoning lie.

Four of Cups, Direct or Inverted

This card refers to dreams and illusions; in a cursing context, it can indicate someone has imagined something about you and is acting on that instead of seeking objective facts. This card (and most cups) also suggests a decision made while inebriated.

Five of Cups, Direct

The Waite-Smith version of this card shows a single person standing in a circle of upset cups. This card appearance illustrates a devastating loss. People heavily grieving death or a lost friendship can manifest this card's emotional energy as much as anyone grieving a failed romance. When this card appears in a cursing diagnostic, look for someone with nothing left to lose.

Seven of Cups, Direct

This card has diverging layers of meaning. The Seven of Cups has more of the air element in it than any card in the suit. Because it refers to illusion, it can be the ultimate card of curse disconfirmation. That said, it may also refer to a vulnerable emotional state that leaves you open to absorbing external negative energy and bad ideas.

Pentacles (Earth)

The earth suit shows what's at stake or what goals the person casting wants to block. It may also show the resources a person has to put into their work against you, so take heed as the higher numbers appear in this arcana.

Three of Pentacles, Inverted

When this card appears, someone believes you violated an agreement. The contract may extend far beyond the financial. Look at the surrounding cards to determine the nature of the broken promise.

Six of Pentacles, Direct and Inverted

The key phrase of this card is "entitlement to authority." Someone perceives themselves as an authority and has decided that they, rather than the universe, should determine what abundance you receive and when. These people can be tricky to root out because their entitlement causes them to see their actions as justice rather than cursing. If this card appears inverted, someone is trying to make bids on what the universe gives you, but the universe won't buy in so long as you speak up and make it clear you reject this person's authority.

Seven of Pentacles, Direct

The Seven of Pentacles suggests two possibilities in a cursing context: either someone dug deep into who you are, or you dug yourself a hole. To me, this card's key message is "you reap what you sow." The card asks you to look at your behavior patterns: if the same problems keep recurring, do you recognize how you contribute to those patterns? Do you acknowledge wrongdoing and make amends to those you have wronged? Do you apologize, no matter how vulnerable and awkward it makes you feel? Look closely at your self, because you did something that *really* made someone mad. In its worst aspects, this card can represent what conjure-folk describe as "crossing you up at the roots." In the worst case, this card may show someone burying a poppet of you or some other working in the soil. The person may be resting over their work, but they indeed did some work on you or who you are reading for! (Don't worry too much; even graveyard spells can break if you're willing to put in the effort.)

Nine of Pentacles, Direct

This card usually indicates someone who wants to "have it all," including your stuff. That attitude often has a great deal of envy and jealousy connected to it, like someone who wants a desired lover all to themselves.

Ten of Pentacles, Inverted

This card indicates someone systemically disrupting every part of your life. Because ten is a number of completion, reversing that energy suggests someone worked to make everything around you fall apart.

Upon performing divination to determine what befell you, you most likely encountered one of the following: a binding, a crossing, a generalized stealing of luck, or a more complex hex with the details somewhat obscured. Each of these can be broken, and in the case of especially persistent nastiness, you may need to do as was done unto you to prevent further problems.

Bindings

Binding is far more controversial than it should be. After the 1996 movie *The Craft* featured a binding, the general public came to associate them with curses or, at the very least, a means of interfering with free will. Bindings do not work like curses and have little bearing on mental influence. A person under a binding can still try to do what they wish. However, you have vastly reduced that entity's chances of succeeding at what you bound them from doing. For example, someone might try to spread rumors that you run a chicken fighting ring—but if you did your job well, somehow those rumors will never affect you or your peaceful urban coop. Under a binding, that person might talk all day long about your chickens at the local diner, but not one person will pay them any attention.

A good binding takes some skill. Beginner bindings tend to come with sweeping declarations of intent, such as "I bind you from harming others." Because absolute harmlessness is virtually impossible in material reality, it renders such workings toothless. Over the years, I have adjusted my bindings' intentions to increase rather than reduce freedom for both myself and the target. I now frame my statement of intent to adjust the connections between us, so their metaphorical fireballs (or whatever they use) miss me. Often, I bind someone's energetic connection out of mine. Essentially we live in parallel universes and no energy between us crosses paths. In this way, they can attempt to pelt me with their anger to their heart's content, and I get to carry on with my life as though the attack doesn't exist.

Spell: Classic Poppet Binding

Fans of the movie *The Craft* know what a classic poppet binding looks like: sew a little doll, stuff it with herbs appropriate to the intention, then wrap it in thread or yarn until it looks like a cocoon in almost cartoonish-looking bondage. The idea is that you psychically tie someone up, ideally until they come to their senses.

Speaking your intention as you wrap your poppet makes a significant difference in how the binding manifests. It allows you to tweak it far more than if you simply threw your "Sit! Stay!" emotions into your work without further instruction.

If I find that a situation merits this type of binding—a binding meant to halt a behavior altogether—I spend extra time crafting my statement of intention first. For each poppet, I compose a phrase that creates a barrier to the results of their actions. As I wind the thread around the effigy, I acknowledge the emotional issues that led to a binding. Those emotional energies activate the spell. If the person's negative emotions about me exceed a certain frequency and volume, the binding fires. As I work a binding, I may say, "I am setting a boundary here. You can have all the feelings you have about me, but I am stopping those emotions' energy from reaching me. Your feelings are yours to take care of."

If I sense someone believes they are doing the right thing, I may express empathy for their discomfort with my choices as I perform the binding. After empathizing, I state what I do isn't about them and that they need to mind their own business. (It's amazing the number of magic workers who are busybodies.)

The following phrases are ones I like to use as I work:

> *"I bind you to yourself—may all*
> *your efforts reach only you."*

> *"I bind you so that you are too busy*
> *with your own life to pester me."*
>
> *"I bind you so that your attempts*
> *at disruption miss every time."*

Only in the case of someone I consider truly dangerous do I add the compelling phrasing:

> *"I bind you from taking action against me*
> *or against those you might choose to harm."*

After you wrap your poppet, you have choices as to what to do with it. To get the person out of your life for good, throw it in running water. To stop actions for the short term, place the doll in a freezer. For a more watchful process, give the poppet a little bed or coffin and check in on it after the person represented calms down.

When ready to dispose of any poppets not thrown into volcanoes or rivers, brush them with ammonia powder to "switch off" the connection and bury the material.

Spell: Bind Two Troublemakers Together

When I have two or more people giving me trouble, I sometimes gift them to one another.

Causing two people who give me grief to make each other suffer might fall into the "evil witch" category of behaviors. When irritated long enough, I turn people who treat me like an enemy against each other. This tendency would ideally warn others to leave me alone, but some people learn by experience instead of observation.

Years ago, when running a volunteer organization, I often found myself working with two or more "problem children." These people stirred up drama, had constant low-stakes complaints, and never followed through on whatever it was they had agreed to do.

One person tried to tell people he ran the organization while I was in charge of it and that no one should talk to me about whatever they were doing! Meanwhile, people were dismissive of my concerns, in part because I was the only woman with a leadership position in the group. Since the people I worked with did not believe me, I found a way to subject them to my experience.

I came up with a project that appealed to my problem child and the group member who had been the most vocally dismissive of my experience. I am not privy to all the details, but I noticed a turnaround in attitude toward me in a very short time. After this project was completed, the dismissive person was much more inclined to believe me when I mentioned a troubling experience. The problem child, now held accountable by someone he considered an equal, quit the organization. Achieving this result with people causing me issues on a practical level led to some ideas about handling this in the spiritual world.

The answer came with a great visual: give my magickal troublemakers a face full of each other!

YOU WILL NEED:

Two paper doll poppets

A pen

A piece of your hair

String or thread

A lemon (optional)

A knife (optional)

On each of the paper dolls, write the name of the person sending you negativity. If you don't know the person, write "troublemaker #1" on one and "troublemaker #2" on the other. Place your hair on top of one of the dolls. Your hair will cause the doll to act as a decoy, making them read the other person as your signature.

Lay one poppet on top of the other with the hair in between them. Wind the thread around the packet. If necessary, fold the dolls into tiny squares. You may want to say something as you bind, such as "I tie you to the other, I entangle you together, you are each other's trouble, and you can stop it, or you're stuck forever."

If you wish, you can then slit the lemon with a knife and stuff the packet in, then throw it in your freezer. The pair will be stuck sending negative energy to each other thinking it's you until you have mercy and take the packet and/or lemon out of your freezer.

Spell: Binding Out
A bind-out may be one of the least intrusive and most effective practices I have for dealing with difficult people. If someone is up in my business and sending me bad energy instead bettering either of us, I remove their energy from mine.

To do this, I grab a piece of paper, a pen, and a spool of thread. On one half of the paper, I write the offender's name. I write my name on the same side of the paper across from the other name. I tear the paper in half between the two names and then fold and wrap the name of the offending person in the thread while saying, "I bind your energy out of mine; this ends any way that we might combine." When finished, I simply throw the bound paper into the garbage. Should we happen to cross paths, that person no longer exists in my world.

I tuck my name paper away in a box or envelope. I may anoint the paper with protection oil, add powder, or insert symbols and charms to block any attempted kickback or binding breakage.

Spell: Bind Out a Situation

While ultimately any given magickal attack comes down to a people problem, there's a point where that problem has enough individuals involved to become a weather condition rather than a specific, targeted attack. Such attacks usually result from toxic gossip chains, such as when a church group decides to "pray for you" and conjure a cloud of their spite in the process. I have heard practitioners versed in psychic attack insist when it's the many against the one, the target is screwed. I refuse to buy into this because I have survived and overcome such attacks.

There are a series of approaches you can take when you become a group target. Do some reconnaissance. Try to identify the group's nature, whether what they send comes from creating a group mind over months and years or if a gossip cloud absorbed enough energy to change into a psychic weather front. Divination can help with this; often, the higher self can tell you everything.

What works best for group pressure often depends on a situation's dynamic. In most cases, you can use the bind out method listed above. Write down the situation, write down your name, tear yourself out of it, and bind that energy out. However, sometimes the situation can be more nuanced than what a simple bind-out can resolve. More people together can create more complications and end-runs around your defenses. You might need to add other spells or energy work to the bind-out to ensure effectiveness in getting the group to leave you alone. Freezing and banishing spells pair well with these works.

Nature abhors a vacuum: if you bind out one energy, another one of similar quality might fill in the blank unless you explicitly call for a positive replacement. Have a positive spell ready to go after the bind out. The spell might be nothing more than asking the universe to fill in the blank with peace.

The following reference provides common group situations that could call for a bind out. Some of you might get extreme and add political parties, the Illuminati, your mother-in-law's bridge club—be aware that you need to be sure they are entangling you before you attempt any magick. You never know who else practices or has psychic sensitivities; a binding might attract someone's attention and make you an additional enemy if you guess wrong. Bridge clubs can get vicious!

Situation: Workplace bind-outs

Symptoms: Low morale; general bad mood in an entire workgroup, cases where one specific person is NOT identifiable as the issue. A general sense of confusion or dizziness walking in or out of the building.

Recommendation: Bind yourself out of the corporate egregore. There's no way, given the existence of corporate espionage, that someone doesn't use large scale witchcraft on corporations to make their environments silos of depression. You can do this by finding a letterhead or printing an image of the corporate logo. Print out the logo, write your name next to it on the piece of paper, and bind as normal. If you hate your company, flush the logo piece down the toilet. For your name paper, get yourself an air cleansing plant like a day lily and bury it in the soil for continuous protection.

Situation: Church Group/Prayer Group Targeting You

Symptoms: Feelings of being under siege. Those who tend to feel textures/sensations psychically note a full-bodied feeling that seems like ill-intended white light.

Recommendation: For this situation, you will likely need to do more, but as a stopgap, you will need a bible or whatever holy book they use. Some Pagans believe that Christian magic has no power; this is folly if you look at most Western cultures. If you know the name of the church or the prayer group, it will help. If you cannot bring yourself to damage a book, skip this spell and pray to archangel Michael for deliverance instead. You need someone from the other "team" to get you out of this and realize that when it comes to the cosmos, there are no tribes or teams. Everybody has magick, whether they call it that or not.

Open the bible to Psalm 100. Rip out the page (or take a picture and print out the copy—but it needs to originate from a physical copy because of the linked energy). Write your name on top of the Psalm text. Write the name of the group praying against you on the other side. Burn it or dissolve it in vinegar if needed. Tie the bible with a black ribbon, stating that the Holy Word is the Word of Love, and no divine weapon may be used against you. Stash the Bible in a safe, dark place.

Situation: Coven targeting you

Symptoms: Nightmares. Night hag/sleep paralysis. General spooky feeling to your household. Feelings of tugging, poking, something invisible getting thrown at you, sense of strings on your head. Doors, windows, doorknobs, and hinges feeling physically strange to the touch.

Recommendation: Remember that you are *not* doomed!

Coveners sometimes fail to account for how their personal opinions and emotions affect a deliberately formed group mind. Some covens never attain a full awareness of their group mind, causing psychic attacks and other problems for people who want to leave the group.

Perform a cut and clear on each member of the coven that you interact with. Second, perform a cut and clear on the coven egregore.

It's a good precaution to burn or otherwise release anything else that came from that coven.

But where's the bind-out? In this case, it's you. Write your name on a slip of paper. Wrap it in blue, black, or silver thread. As you do, see yourself moving to a dimension outside the reach of the coven. You may inhabit the world simultaneously but will inhabit it at a different frequency so they can no longer reach you.

Situation: Clique/group of friends/former friends

Symptoms: You may feel "strings" on your head and/or as though you are being watched. Often there's a synchronicity/stalking feeling. Sink taps turn on at night after they were shut off.[1]

Recommendation: Perform cut and clears. Consider anyone you are still friends with who might inadvertently link you to them. Cast a stop gossip spell.

---

1. The faucet phenomenon specifically has happened to people I know as well as myself during periods of psychic attack.

While the above series does not cover every situation, it does list some of the more common sources of group/giant attack and what to do. Other, more subtle magick can also affect your life while not necessarily registering as an attack. For example, an ex may work a reconciliation spell on you. While that might not trigger wards, it may also do harm in a different way, so pay close attention to your own emotions, especially if you find yourself suddenly changing your mind about someone without any real reason to do so.

Freezing

Freezing spells have the elegance of saying to the uncouth parts of the universe, "just stop!" But the practice halts more than just activities against you—it can also halt improvements to the situation. Craft your intention with extreme finesse. Freezing often leaves the target in exactly that place in *every aspect of their life* until you release them. If it's a coworker, that person will stay in the same position. If it's an ex-lover, they will not heal and move on from you. A bad neighbor may stay next door. All the habits and mentality of the person frozen remain the same because these spells also halt personal growth. Please make sure you release the spell/take it out of the freezer once you achieve your objective. Even if that person doesn't have the capacity for growth, stagnation can turn into rot, which risks causing much larger issues.

Spell: Lemon Freezer
In this spell, the lemon traps the energy of your troublemaker and sours any of their attempts on your peace. It also acts as a container for other energies you might want to weave in to your "knock if off!" message. For example, if I want the target to calm

down, I might stuff the lemon with a few pieces of valerian root or lavender buds.

YOU WILL NEED:

One lemon

A knife

A picture or a piece of paper with someone's name on it

Foil or plastic for wrapping the lemon

Cut a cross-shaped hole in the lemon, making sure to pierce the skin but not pierce the lemon on the other side. Stuff your name paper or picture through the slit. Add anything else you wish to fit to tweak your spell outcome. I favor adding a pinch of alum crystal for its gossip-stopping properties, but you can add any small object as intuition guides and as the lemon can hold. Wrap the lemon in foil or plastic and place it in your freezer.

The lemon is best kept in an opaque container slid to the back of your freezer, thus preventing your housemates from disturbing the lemon on the way to a popsicle.

Spell: Paper Freezer

The paper freezer spell works on the same principles as the lemon freezer spell. The difference between the spells lies in how its structure affects the person named. While the lemon adds a souring effect, paper in water just sends a signal to chill out. I've used it on coworkers that liked to direct their hostility at me with great success. Rather than dodge them or their mood swings, I sometimes just scribbled their name on a piece of paper, slid it into an empty ice cube tray, poured water over it, and threw it in the freezer.

For days when I knew we would be working together, I enjoyed a calmer environment. But the "stuck" effect could sometimes make it necessary to take the paper out to thaw. For example, if that person was up for a transfer, that would get them out of my way. Should that happen for you, I recommend throwing their ice cube in a mug and putting it in the microwave for two minutes. Bon voyage and happy trails!

For gentler paper freezing, you can add drops of food coloring to add emotional flavors so the target remains inclined to a certain mood. For instance, if someone tends to have anger issues, adding blue or green for calming might improve the situation. If someone tended towards depression and moodiness, yellow could bolster their sense of optimism. A single drop of red coloring might help that person view coworkers in a more positive light. One caveat: the effect of color magick changes based on a person's culture. Make sure you know how your target may interpret a color before applying it in spell work.

Spell: Fire and Ice Spell to Break a Freezing

If you suspect or know that someone froze you, don't worry—you can break out of it. Burning an uncrossing candle and taking cleansing baths help this, but if you want something that moves a little bit faster, try the following.

YOU WILL NEED:

A slip of paper with your name

A cube of frozen lemon juice (prepare in an ice cube tray)

1 T sugar

A tea light candle

A heat-safe bowl

Place the name paper on the bottom of the bowl, with the lemon ice cube on top. Top the ice with a generous spoonful of white sugar. Take the tea light candle out of its container and set it on top of the ice cube and sugar. Light the candle. If it burns down before the ice melts, light a second candle. Repeat this spell once a day until you feel your life moving forward again.

Reversals

Reversal spells, like bindings, have an abundance of superstition and overthinking applied to them. Some people think it might reverse every positive working they've ever done or invite a massive setback. I have also come across people who believe giving people their negative energy back should stop their bad behavior. Usually, putting someone on the receiving end of their cruelty *does* persuade them to stop, but some people take this as an invitation to war. Think carefully and perform divination to scan for the likely impact and consequences of a reversal.

To me, reversal is a flexible concept that can include the concepts of sending the negativity back: "rewind that," "reset that," and "turn that inside out." I lean into these interpretations of the word when crafting my reversal spell intentions.

Spell: Classic Reversal

A classic reversal is also known as a return to sender spell. It does what it sounds like: grabs the energy someone directs to you and bounces it back. In theory, the sender experiences whatever they planned for you. In most cases, people stop what they're doing when it gets dished back to them.

You can perform a bounce-back reversal spell in a variety of simple ways. If the problem is especially persistent, combine the following methods to see what gets satisfying results.

YOU WILL NEED:

One black candle, glass jar or taper is fine

A barbecue skewer or small knife or marker

Reversal oil (recipe at the end of this section)

A mirror that can stand behind the candle

On one side of the candle, carve or write the words "return to sender." Anoint the wick with reversal oil and set a mirror behind the candle. Light the candle and allow it to burn down. Make doubly sure you use fire safety protocols for any reversal spell, whether it means standing the candle in a huge metal bucket or burning the candle inside a fireproof safe. Reversal spells tend to have the wildest energy of all common candle spells; breaks and flame bursts happen with them more frequently.

Spell: Hand Gesture Reversal

If you feel safe enough to physically touch the energy sent, responding to it with whatever hand gesture means "go away" in your cultural lexicon works effectively. Sadly, the middle finger does not work for this, likely due to overuse.

My most common shooing gesture is to hold out my projective hand, thumb under four fingers, palm down. I lift my four fingers while imagining launching the sent energy back at the sender. I may even say, "shoo!" out loud. In such moments, I imagine myself as an especially badass granny witch. Nobody messes with granny!

The Double-Action Reversal Candle

If you frequent botanicas and advanced-practitioner occult shops, you have seen this tool, seven-day glass jar candles half-filled with two colors of wax. The different color combinations address different flavors of reversals.[2] The bottom color represents the energy banished/driven out, and the top color represents the type of energy being returned/pushed back to the originator. Red and black is the most common combination. Some magick workers believe black on top provides a more forceful returning of energy, but I have found little relationship between color order and strength of impact.

Other colors veer away from what countermagick calls for but can come in handy for unique situations you might want to turn around. Color correspondence charts for candles are freely available online. While most feature black for half the candle and any other color as the other half, you'll sometimes find other pairings such as red with pink or green with yellow. For countermagick and hex twisting, this short chart assumes black is always the color of the top half of the candle.

Reversal Candle Color Chart
Red: protection, turning around negative energy and attacks
Green: reversing bad financial luck and circumstances
Blue: reversing poor health, restoring peace
Purple: reversing domination, correcting a toxic balance of power
Yellow: restoring hope, removing mental poisoning
Pink: reconciliation, reversing damage from emotional fights

---

2. This is not the only use for double-action candles—they can be used for almost any energy inversion, be it for love, money, or switching psychic talents on and off.

You can assign personal meanings to the colors to refine your intent.

Spell: The Double-Action Reversal Candle Working

First, wipe off your candle. Glass jar candles can sit on store shelves for a long time and often need a dusting. In some traditions, wiping them with Florida Water or a similar cleanser is especially appropriate. After removing the dust, write directions or symbols on the glass around your candle with a marker. Select the color of your marker based on how you want the recipient to feel. Black and grey markers help stop a person from realizing what's happening. Pink sends it back with a smile. Red comes with some force. Yellow heightens self-awareness, but be cautious when using it. Self-awareness sometimes increases a person's aggression. If the person has little self-awareness already, the response will be immediate and harsh.

If you wish, dress and load your candles. If you put enough energy into your candle, you never need do any dressing or decorate, although the practice does help you refine your spell's intention. Loading a candle involves poking holes in the wax with a chopstick or barbecue skewer and filling them with appropriate oil(s). It is likely you can buy a reversal oil at the shop where you purchased the candle.

If you prefer to make your own, this is my go-to recipe:

Recipe: Reversal Oil

This go-to oil gets used most in candle spells, charm bags, and petitions. You can also apply it to your finger and then trace symbols and sigils in the air where you want the opposite to happen, or when you want to cancel the impact of something happening.

YOU WILL NEED:

One small chunk of dragon's blood (oil soluble)

One sliver of a cinnamon stick

Two cloves

A pinch of black pepper

Olive oil

Rue or eucalyptus, one pinch each (optional)

Add all material to a small bottle. Add olive oil after dry herbs. Allow the ingredients to sit in a cool, dark place and shake once a day for two weeks. When ready for use, strain the herbs and rebottle. If you need to use the oil before a fortnight has expired, add a pinch of rue or eucalyptus herb to the formula.

Spell: Opposites Day

Rather than return bad energy sent my way, sometimes I welcome it. Good or bad, energy is all usable material. Where some people might see a pile of worn-out old socks, others might see potential pillow stuffing. You can choose to look at the negative energy someone is sending you as a gross and dirty thing—*or* a generous gift. Once you get comfortable accepting ill-intended energy with an intention to transform it, you level up. Depending on what I can discern of the intention sent toward me, I might tweak what happens. When that nasty energy lands, I declare, "It's Opposites Day!" All that's necessary to make this happen is a standard reversal candle. As you put your energy into it, tell it, "Receive the negative energy ... and make it the opposite. Illness is good health; failure is a success; despair is joy."

The argument could be made that this approach is one of the few that helps everyone involved. Your sender vents the issues they're projecting onto you, and instead of hurting your life, they improve it.

Spell: Reversal-Redirect

This spell forwards energies sent to you elsewhere, to a place of your choosing, much like forwarding phone calls or email.

First, decide where you want the energy or spirits to go. The simple option is delivering it to a body of water. If you do not already have a relationship with a river or ocean, visit the nearest body of water to your home. Introduce yourself, sing to it, and bring an offering such as a flower. Then explain your intention of sending it these energies. If you make a promise to this water, keep it. Animistic spirits have the most time to remember everything. If you feel comfortable doing something more advanced (that is, riskier), you can also find a spirit who wants the energy for themselves. I prefer to supply this energy to crossroads spirits as an offering. They are always wheeling and dealing, so giving them more tools to cut deals makes them happy, not to mention that unloading what I don't want makes *me* happy. In some situations, the energy is so tainted that spirits refuse it; what to do in those situations is covered later.

YOU WILL NEED:

A lava lamp or something that has a similar relaxing/trippy effect when watched (seriously)

A vessel with a lid that seals

A white, red, or black candle

A small bowl with honey, your picture, and some of your hair

A metal tray

Optionally, a magnet

This spell functions as a honey trap for the energy/attention of whoever wants to send you badness. The lava lamp captivates the attention of any delivering spirits (including fire elementals that originate in someone else's lit candles). With their attention diverted, they fall in the jar, you trap them, and then you can burn off the energy in the sun or leave the jar open in the morning for a spirit with whom you have a collection pact.

Unless you can obtain a battery-operated lava lamp, you will need to set it near an electrical outlet. Lava lamps can be fire hazards, so proceed with caution.

To prepare, dress the candle to attract the bad things to you. You may even want to use attraction or love oils. As you prepare it, make comments aloud about how happy you are and how great everything is going. On a tray, set the candle in the bowl with the honey and your hair. Put the vessel next to it. Set the lamp so that it stands behind both the tray and the vessel. When you go to bed each night, turn on the lava lamp and uncap the vessel. Each morning, replace the lid. When ready to empty the vessel, uncap it and leave it in direct sunlight—the sun will burn off the remaining energy, or a spirit you made an agreement with will come collect that energy. If you opted to give the energy to a spirit, put out an offering, like a shot of rum, when you invite the entity to collect. Reset the trap each evening before bed as needed.

Spell: Situation Reversal

Sometimes everything goes bad all at once; with such an enormity of chaos, it's hard to pin down what's weather and what's people actively causing trouble. In many ways, this spell isn't so much countermagick; it counters life patterns instead of magick.

I recommend this most often when two people in the same home lose jobs at the same time or when a slew of little problems occur.

Again, in this arena of magick, it is all about intention. One way to signify intention is through the symbols you apply. For example, if you use a marker to write on glass candles, you might use the rewind symbol (<<) instead of typical arrows (← or →). Rather than use the common directional symbol screen-printed on reversal candles traditionally with a single vertical line and an arrow pointing outwards on each end, I use something from contemporary technology: the rewind button. The back arrow is also a signal to spirit to rewind your situation and then rewrite it. Essentially, it sends a message: "Back up; this doesn't all need to be happening."

This spell usually manifests in a way that moves you forward in your life. You probably won't get your old job back, and your truck won't come back to life, but you will find you have a new job or that whatever you lost was replaced. The crises stop. After you set this spell, I recommend following up with a cleansing and protection working if they are not part of your routine practice. If you lost money, cast a spell to draw money your way for good measure.

YOU WILL NEED:

One double-action reversal candle, half red and half black. If you cannot obtain one, a plain white candle with the bottom half covered in aluminum foil works fine

A black marker

Fire safety protocol

Reversal oil

Write your name and any details of your situation on the candle with the marker. Add the rewind symbol (<<), if appropriate.

Anoint the wick and the upper lip of the glass with reversal oil. Place in a safe place, and before you light the candle, state out loud that you would like this stream of bad luck to turn around and into improvement.

Working: Collecting Ammo

You can store metaphysical energy just like fuel can be stored in a cell. If done well, it doesn't matter if the energy comes in as good or bad. If someone insists upon sending you nastiness, pick a container to collect it. From there, you can send it through a filter or transmutation and say to your detractor, "Awesome! How generous of you to provide me with all this energy and attention! I can't wait to use this to my ends!"

YOU WILL NEED:

A mason jar with a two-piece lid

A picture of yourself, some hair, a used bandage of yours, etc.

A handful of pea-sized gravel (collect this from a driveway or buy it from a craft store if you must)

Salt, white, nothing fancy

An LED tea light candle

Optional: Attraction oil, magnet oil, or lodestone oil

At the bottom of the jar, place your photo and the DNA. Anoint a few gravel pieces with attraction or magnet oil, visualizing that gravel absorbing the energy targeting you. Fill the jar about three-quarters full of gravel. Next, think of the salt as a means of transmutation. Imagine the salt leaching out the negative energy that comes into the jar, acting as an antiseptic. Leave the solid part of the mason jar lid on the bottom, but screw the ring portion onto the jar. Place the LED light on top of the stack and switch it on. Because I take glee in silliness, I sometimes set this while yelling, "Come and get it!" or "Over here, stupid!"

Leave until the LED light burns out, unscrew the mason jar lid ring and add the solid cover. When you need extra energy for another spell, take out one of the gravel pieces and place it close to your other spell components, so it provides power. If you have no other spells to cast, let the pea gravel rest with a houseplant or on a sunny windowsill.

Working: Removing Tainted Energy

The natural world is the magickal world, and that includes both medicines and poisons. Sometimes what someone sends has so much negative energy in it that it needs more than a reversal. If you are in a situation that results in such tainted energy, you will likely need to see a healer or shaman. Since it can take time to find the right person, the following energy filter will reduce the impact of hard-to-purify energy until you find the right person to aid you.

YOU WILL NEED:

A mason jar with a two-piece lid

A magnet (a small refrigerator magnet is fine for this)

A little bit of your hair or DNA as you desire

Baking soda

Water (tap water is fine)

Cheesecloth

A piece of obsidian (you can enhance the obsidian by putting it next to tourmaline, and if you can get one, a septarian crystal)

Wrap your hair around the magnet and drop it in the jar. Add two teaspoons of baking soda and fill the jar three-quarters full of water. Place the cheesecloth over the jar and tighten the screw cap over it. Set the obsidian on top of the cheesecloth and position the jar next to your reversal candle or healing working, where the jar will act as a "filter" on the energy that the candle moves. Once a day, flush the water and refill with fresh water, placing the obsidian back on top of the cheesecloth. The negative energy gets filtered through the obsidian and the baking soda, neutralizing the worst of the muck, ultimately making it more useful to the spirits willing to take it.

Revocations

Revocation is a practice used in saint worship. It effectively sucks bad or malevolent energy out of your home or away from you, trapping it so you can dispose of it safely. It is also a spell requiring skill with your hands and may test your fire safety needs.

Working: Revoke Bad Energy

I once had to perform this working at a party; its effects were so immediate that my usually skeptical friend commented, "woo, I felt all the bad stuff sucked right out of me!" Practice flipping the full cup of water onto the plate over the sink—it takes some practice not to get water everywhere!

YOU WILL NEED:

A full glass of water

A glass, ceramic, or metal plate

A lighter

One white Shabbat candle

Take the glass and put the plate over the top. Flip it over quickly, relying on centrifugal force to keep the water in. The upside-down glass of water represents an inversion of negative energies and intentions sent into the home. Using the lighter, melt the bottom of the Shabbat candle to stick on top of the glass.

Traditionally, prayer is addressed to Archangel Michael before lighting the candle, asking for a revocation of all evil directed at you. Praying to angels works fine in most situations, as long as you get along with them. Not everyone gets on well with angels. Fortunately, other entities can and will help with this spell. You may address the prayer to your ancestors, to deities you worship, or simply call upon spirit and/or nature iself to revoke all negativity from your household. Light the candle. Once it burns down, carefully take the water to a sink or a houseplant and pour it out: the negative energy is gone and ready to be rinsed away. Scrape all the wax off the glass and wash it along with the plate.

Most of the spells in this chapter act as metaphysical dog-poo cleaners. Someone left something nasty, and now you just need to clean it, shoo it, or give it back. Unless you gain the attention of a magickal pro or live in a place of multiple improbable tragedies, just keeping your home and life clean does plenty to keep you safe. Save revocation for more dire situations.

Working: Flame Free Revocation

While nothing beats the flipped-glass revocation method (in my opinion), not everyone can light candles for their magick. When you want to revoke negativity sent at you but can't light a candle, set up the spell with the flipped glass as above and instead of a candle, place a rare earth magnet and LED candle on top of it. This still calls the energy your way and gives it it a light to find you—and importantly, still leads it into that water trap of the inverted glass.

SEVEN

HEALTH PROTECTION
Spells to Ward and Preserve the (Energetic) Bodies

It's always a good idea to protect your health because you share the world with billions of invisible beings. It's easy to get hit with a bug because germs abound in the material world, and that common knowledge can work against a spiritually beleaguered person. When someone wants to take us down, making us sick is always the most accessible avenue. Along with maintaining good hygiene practices—don't just wash your hands, moisturize them!—giving your immunity a little extra boost via magick can always help.

Working: Health Preserving Mojo Bag

Valerie Worth's *Crone's Book of Words* has my favorite version of a charm bag. The following bundle spell is certainly inspired by it and uses some of the same ingredients. To make your own, choose a green, blue, or red cloth. While many spells call for flannel, silk, or velvet, it's more about using what's available. I often cut up a piece of clothing I no longer wear for this purpose; old T-shirts come in especially handy for this.

You can make a bag from this cloth by folding over a rectangle and stitching two opposite sides, leaving the top open for adding the herbs. I prefer to use black thread, but you can adjust your color choice according to what aspect of your health the bag is related to. If you hate sewing, don't worry, there is a no-sew method: place the herbs in the center of a square piece cloth and fold the fabric up so that it forms a bag that you can tie off with thread. Fabric glue also works if you plan to only handle your bag every few days.

Place in the center of the cloth one clove of garlic, a few juniper berries, any cedar tree needles you can find, and a few cloves. Carry the bag on your person and anoint daily with any health or healing oil.

Recipe: Immunity Enhancing Incense (Maximum Strength)

Use this to give your personal energy a little boost during periods of stress. While designed for burning over incense charcoal, you can also omit the resins and boil the bay, juniper, and thyme over the stove for a scented steam. You need not burn the incense mix, especially if you have smoke allergies. In addition to boiling the mixture on your stovetop, another option is to make a tincture of it with potable alcohol to be added to a steam-based essential oil diffuser. You may opt to make a potion and use the herbal mixture as a spray. The point of incense is to get it into the atmosphere; it doesn't *need* to burn to work as intended.

YOU WILL NEED:

Bay leaves

Benzoin (powdered)

Frankincense (powdered)

Juniper berries

Thyme

Mix the herbs and resins in equal parts. If you need exact measurements, begin by adding one teaspoon of herb at a time. While I advise that you powder the resins before using them in a bag, do not powder the herbs. If you crush herbs with a mortar and pestle, do so just enough to activate the volatile oils but no more.

Burn a pinch of this mixture on incense charcoal in a heat-proof container. Some people might question using incense for health issues, and that's a valid concern. Please see the previous steam recipe offered as an alternative if needed. Smoke cleanses in a different way from steam, which is why incense burning has so much tradition behind it. Of course, the practice was more common in a time when we did not have the building materials we now use to keep insects and other critters out of our homes.

You can add this incense to any other working or simply burn it and use it as a focal point while praying for your health and wellness.

Recipe: Disease Expelling Powder

The following recipe calls for an animistic perspective. If you see illnesses as spirits, you can persuade those spirits to leave. This expulsion powder makes it so that the illness's intelligence must go and take all its children with it. Use this when your entire household seems beset with stubborn, long-term illnesses.

YOU WILL NEED:

1 t calamus

1 t coriander

1 t juniper

1 t myrrh

1 T baking soda

1 T cornstarch

Grind all the herbal ingredients as finely as you can. While some like to use the mortar and pestle in the belief that it adds more power, I find a food processor or a coffee grinder designated for herbs extremely convenient. If the ground herb feels weak after a run through a grinder, If the ground herb feels weak after a go through a grinder, you can always add power after pulverization. Pray to your protective deities and healing spiritual authorities to drive out all illness and banish curses, hexes, and the like along the way. Store the resulting powder in an old but thoroughly washed and dried vitamin or pill bottle.

When someone falls ill, take a makeup brush and dust this on your doorways and windows. Sprinkle some under the doormats. Pay special attention to the bathroom and kitchen or any other areas that several people use; these areas traffic a lot of germs! This gives a small boost to the standard precautions of washing and drying hands, covering your mouth when you sneeze, and keeping clean air circulating as much as possible.

Milagros for Health Protection

Milagros are charms that folk-Catholicism practitioners from around the world place on their home altars. Each charm symbolizes an intention or expression of gratitude. In the case of a health charm, it might include a medallion of Saint Raphael for fierce healing, a tiny pair of scissors to represent cutting off negativity, and so on.

You can purchase pre-made milagros kits (including charms) in most botanicas. Be aware that if you don't understand the symbols in a Christian context, they may not work as well for you. You might wish to make your own milagros from scratch, choosing charms and symbols that have meaning to you. What I'm recommending for a health chain is based on my general practice. While you can buy charms from a jewelry supplier, you could also make them out of paper or clay to truly customize them to your own needs.

On a red string, tie the following charms:

- A medallion of Saint Michael (for fierce protection)
- An apple (to symbolize continued nurturance and health)
- A heart (for emotional and physical health)
- A key (representing mastery of your body and spirit)
- A lock (representing protection from what might cross your boundaries)
- A Willendorf goddess (for ample health and energy at any size)
- A five-pointed star (for the protection of the elements)
- A zodiac charm representing your sun sign
- A zodiac charm representing your moon sign

You can wear this like a charm bracelet or add it to your mojo bag. Pray over it and anoint it with health oil daily. You can also use the following spoken charm to reinforce its power:

> *Protect me from the heavens with the heavens*
>
> *Protect me from the earth with the earth*
>
> *Protect me from plants with plants*
>
> *Protect me from the air with air*
>
> *Protect me from the soil with soil*
>
> *Protect me from the past with the past*
>
> *Protect me from the future with the future*
>
> *Within and without, out and throughout*
>
> *May the power that guards me render weak and powerless all magic of gods and humanity to harm me, to bring me down, to bring my body down!*
>
> *Amen/So Mote It Be*

Recipe: Health and Healing Oil

Use this oil to dress healing candles or anoint your charms and bags, or add a few drops on pillows or to your wash. Don't use this for a spell you want to work on tonight—herbs can take about three weeks to infuse. Let them macerate in peace. When the time comes and after straining the oil, add essential oils and wait a day for them to blend fully.

YOU WILL NEED:

  2 clean glass jars with lids

  1 to 2 T angelica, chopped

  1 to 2 T rue, chopped

1 to 2 T calamus, chopped

1 to 2 T life everlasting, chopped

1 to 2 T eucalyptus, chopped

1 to 2 T agrimony, chopped

Sunflower oil

Cheesecloth

4 drops juniper essential oil

3 drops lemongrass essential oil

2 drops ginger essential oil

In a clean glass jar, add one to two tablespoons each of the above chopped herbs. Pour sunflower oil over the herbs. Press down with a spoon or chopstick to remove all bubbles. Set in a sunny place to allow the solar heat to infuse the oils—shake once a day. You may wish to add a chant or prayer as you do this. When you smell more herbs than sunflower oil, strain the oil through a cheesecloth into a new glass jar. Again, press down on the herbs with a spoon to extract as much infused oil as possible. A standard strainer does not filter nearly enough of the herbs. Add the essential oils. Shake gently and store in a cool, dry place.

Magickal Inoculation Recipes

One of the most traditional and nastiest ways to affect a cursed person is to target their health, often by using spells that go after bodily fluids, especially the blood. While blood magick can be magick that uses blood as a means of exponentially enhancing power, it also refers to spells that *target* blood. When someone uses a spell aimed at someone's blood, it is a nasty business that uses magickal energy to infect a person's ability to produce the cells that sustain life. These spells can manifest as a result of ingesting something poisonous or entering the energy bodies through sympathetic magic. Such curses often manifest as illness, aches, and pains that defy medical diagnosis. They resemble chronic fatigue syndrome without having any of the DNA markers. If you think this might have happened to you and have already exhausted all medical avenues, you can try the following recipes—but keep advocating for medical help. Please be very aware of how your prescriptions affect you and how they may interact with the following spell ingredients, as they can neutralize some medications.

Both recipes use vinegar; dilute them with water before ingestion. Both are most beneficial after you correct your wards and protections. This way, you and the potion are not fighting off stuff trying to force a backslide.

Recipe: Potion to Cancel Bloodstream Magick

This vinegar tincture becomes more potent over time, but if it's an emergency, you can start a jar today and use it relatively quickly. You can take it as early as an hour after its preparation. Note: Do not use this recipe if you have acid reflux.

YOU WILL NEED:

Clean mason jar with lid, 1 quart

1 C fresh or frozen pomegranate seeds

1 ginger knob chopped but not peeled

Apple, sliced but not peeled, seeded

1 T tarragon vinegar or fire cider (an apple vinegar tincture of hot peppers, garlic, lemons, cloves, and horseradish)

Apple cider vinegar

Chop the ingredients and fill a one-quart mason jar. Pour in the tarragon vinegar or fire cider. Top with apple cider vinegar as needed. Shake well. While you can begin using the mixture after one hour, it is most potent after seven days. Shake the mixture once a day.

> **Dosage:** Add one tablespoon of this potion to one cup of white sage tea. Please be aware that sage does raise body temperature and is contraindicated for pregnancy. If you have a petite body, reduce the sage tea from one cup to one-half cup, leaving the vinegar dosage at one tablespoon.

Recipe: Potion to Inoculate against Blood Magick

An ounce of prevention is worth a pound of cure. Unfortunately, it never occurred to me to inoculate against blood magick specifically until I needed the following potion. Someone going after your blood is, hopefully, a rare occurrence. That said, if you practice magick with any degree of risk, seriously consider this precaution.

This recipe uses an alcohol-based tincture; I prefer to use gin or vodka after running either of the beverages through fish-filter charcoal. If you cannot consume alcohol, white vinegar works just as well. If you don't want to use white vinegar, vegetable glycerin has a shorter shelf life but will deliver the desired effect.

YOU WILL NEED:

Mason jar with lid

Peel from one pomegranate

½ C fresh lavender buds (better if they are still green)

Garlic skins from 2–3 garlic bulbs

½ C dried white sage

Gin, vodka, or white vinegar

Strainer (optional)

As in the blood magick cure recipe, place all the ingredients in the mason jar. Fill to the top with filtered vodka, gin, or vinegar. Shake well. Store in a cool, dry place, shaking once a day for two weeks. After, strain if desired. Add one tablespoon to your preferred beverage or tea. Take one dose daily for three weeks.

EIGHT

SPELLS FOR TAKING IT TO THE MATTRESSES

Finding Out Who Did What and What to Do about Them If They Went Too Far

Negative energy is a normal part of life. Dirt builds up, and then it's time to clean. Sometimes, though, what you're dealing with is not just dirt—it's a mudslide.

If you find yourself in that energetic mudslide, you may need to seek outside help. You know when too much is coming when the condition extends beyond daily bad moods and incidental bad luck. Look for an order of escalation when misfortune occurs. If, for example, you remove a spirit and find a new, more difficult to remove one has found its way in despite proper warding, take it as a sign of a persistent attack. If people being more unpleasant with you for reasons other than what is usual for you, and this goes on for days and weeks, that's another sign.

There is a point at which the trouble won't stop until something stops it. Unless you want to spend months or even years of your life enduring and cleaning up the constant energetic mess, you must fight back.

For some, this leads to a moral quandary: if you live according to the moral principle to harm none or subscribe to doctrines forbidding against interference with free will, you will probably have to reconsider these foundations to defend yourself. If you know you need to shift perspective and struggle with it, you might find it helpful to research who fares better in a physical fight: those who punch back or those who curl up into the fetal position. It seems the people who punch back often get to keep their wallets and a little bit of their dignity *but* only if they fight well. In my opinion, a moral victory does not compensate someone for a broken nose, whether that schnoz is physical, metaphysical, or metaphorical.

Spells to Reveal Enemies

In the first two chapters, I explain how to diagnose negative energy. Often, the question of "whodunit" also comes up during diagnostics. In most cases, the culprit is obvious. It's the coworker who gives you the stink eye, or the father-in-law who always hated you, and so on. Most of the time, it's not even a concentrated spell but the continuous manifestation of emotional energy directed at you.

Sometimes, however, someone puts some thought into the energy they send you. Your father-in-law might have hired a spiritual worker to chase you away from his son. Your coworker might be working a few spells to get that promotion, and one or two of those workings includes making you look terrible to the boss. The world of professional spirit workers is one of nonjudgment in the extreme because all too often, the bad guy in the situation has problems that they might come to us with, too. Many of us are unlikely to quibble about all of someone's moral standing in someone else's daily life drama. We do the client's work before us with the understanding that people often seek out spirit workers for negative work. In some cases, whether the work is negative or positive depends on the side of the working you're on.

We also don't divulge our clients. If someone thought far enough ahead to hire one of us, you may be better off just addressing the energy and not worrying about who it came from.

Knowing the identity of an especially persistent bully does make a lot of magick much easier to reverse. If you're not entirely sure who did it or who specifically is helping someone send you the bad stuff, there are a few methods to learn the identity of your troublemaker, assuming they haven't hired someone to trace it to instead. If the person sending at you doesn't have good shielding, is averse to paying for magickal services, and doesn't have developed skills in spiritual invisibility, the following methods are likely to work well.

Spell: Finding the Name

This spell works best when you know the name or part of the person cursing you. To find this answer, clear your mind and ask, "Who is cursing me?" If you struggle to concentrate, listen to a binaural file to help attain the state of relaxation and concentration that you need, and try again. If you need to move around a lot, consider listening to the files while exercising. For example, I often set information seeking as my intention before yoga practice. Usually, by the end of practice, during savasana (corpse pose), the answer arrives. You need not practice yoga to try this. Set an intention before biking or weight lifting; the answer may well come during your cool-down.

Working: Jana Meditation

While the Roman god Janus (two faces, back to back, open mouth) gets a lot of attention, his counterpart Jana, goddess of passageways. When asked nicely, Jana helps find what someone has hidden from you. While academic writing tends to describe her as a variation of the Roman/Italian Diana, this is not how I have experienced her. To me, she very much has her own energy and does her own powerful thing.

Perform this working at least partially as a ritual of conscious meditation. It works best at night, although I have obtained reasonable results in the daytime that took just a little more energy to get. Doing it when the moon is visible in the sky improves the experience and quality of the results with far less mental strain.

First, set out an offering to Jana. Moon-charged water is good, as are most white wines and pale-colored grape juices. Then make yourself comfortable. I like to lie down on blankets. You might want to sit in a chair or lie on your bed. Choose whatever position allows the clearest interpretation of your own body signals. Say a few words to request Jana's guidance through the doorways of our experience. I prefer to do this work with my eyes closed and follow the visions she leads me through.

Jana tends to arrive nude, with long brown or black hair down to the back of her knees. She is likely to lead you down a dark hallway filled with doors. Be prepared to follow her for a while. Eventually, she will stop at one door and push it open. You will see your enemy and possibly details about the work they are targeting you with.

Ask Jana to show you the secret passageways that lead from this doorway to you. There is a large caveat: you may see that person's spirit-form, meaning they could appear as an animal, a plant, an alien being, or many other possibilities. Take note of how they appear and what that appearance might represent. From there, you can research animal omens and might be able to connect the animal characteristics to people you know.

Spell: The Telltale Heart

This spell is an adaptation from a grimoire that called for an actual animal heart. If you would like to see the original spell, I highly recommending purchasing your own copy of the grimoire. In the original, you hang a cow's heart in your fireplace after sticking pins in it. Suffering torment, your enemy will then confess. Hopefully, those committed to the original edition of this spell will remember to place a drip pan underneath. For everyone else, the following variation works almost as well. The main differences are that you will have to work harder to energize it, it likely hurts less, and this spell is vegan friendly.

YOU WILL NEED:

Construction paper

Scissors

Chalk or a pen, any color

A paper punch

Thread

About ten tea light candles

An image of a magickal seal that compels truth such as the
   Fourth Pentacle of the Sun

Something from which the paper can be suspended, such as
   a stand for fireplace tools

To work this spell, you need a way to suspend the "heart" over a heat source. If you have a fireplace, you can usually rig something in the chimney. However, fireplaces are far less common than they once were, so you may need a variation. First, cut a heart from the construction paper. This component can look like an anatomical heart or like the Valentine type. On one side of the paper, write, "CONFESS, MY ADVERSARIES." On the other side, draw or glue the seal for speaking the truth.

Using a hole-punch, make a hole in the heart. As for placement, if you want the person(s) involved to experience guilt, punch a hole in the paper allowing it to hang with the point of the heart down. If you want to motivate behavior change, place the hole so it points upward. It should, if using a Valentine's shaped heart, resemble a posterior from that perspective. Hold it between your hands, pouring your will and emotional energy into it. The heart should almost jump out of your hands from the vibration.

Hang the heart-piece from your fireplace tool rack or a hanger you can hook over the edge of a metal plant stand. Hang it high enough that the tea light candle won't ignite it. Place the candle where anything nearby feels growing heat but won't burst into flames. Sprinkle a little black pepper around (not on!) the candle to add to the torment.

Let the tea light burn down. Change it once daily until you discover your enemy. The revelation may come in the form of a direct confession or boast. It might also result from their protections and invisibilities melting away, and somehow you know who has been making trouble. When you have your answer, bury the heart or burn it—your choice.

Divination: Multiple Curses/Multiple Enemies

The following tarot spread goes a step beyond the layouts in the diagnostic chapter. The following reading can help you sort out concurrent attacks.

First, shuffle and pull one card—this represents you and where you're at. Next, draw a ring of cards to reveal the influences around you. If you see more than one court card, pull two more cards on each of them. That next card indicates what energy that card is sending you, helping you determine what you might need to clear out. Again, through the characteristics of the cards, you might successfully identify the source of your problems.

How Magickal Invisibility Works

Invisibility serves its purpose primarily as next-level protection: if the world of spirit can't see your works, no one can meddle in them. Learning to make your doings invisible to the spiritual world can save you from interference. On the other hand, it can cause some problems. Knowing how and when to use invisibility magick takes some finesse.

Keep in mind the potential for a misfiring—if you use an invisibility spell to protect your property and open a business, your business might fail because no one notices your shop. If you use it on your person, you may have more people bumping into you, saying, "Sorry, didn't see you there!" On the other hand, those of you who have not wanted your teacher to call on you in class and have successfully projected the "please don't call on me" field know that at the right time and right place, intentional invisibility is awesome.

Unlike in the movies, invisibility does not work by making you translucent/nonreflective in light. Spiritual invisibility functions more like camouflage, matching energy to your surroundings or projecting that your surroundings in some way match you. As to how it might affect others, it will depend on how a person perceives energy. For people that get visions, they may just see black/white/blank space. For someone that hears, they get silence. For those that feel, they might slide past that energy without registering its presence.

In chapter six's passage about reversal work, I talk about the importance of intent, especially when using words with flexible meanings. When it comes to invisibility, it's also important to sift out layered meanings from the ward and set spells accordingly. Because invisibility is in some ways password protection, it also means that you want to control who has access and who does not. Whoever can and can't see what you do depends entirely on how you verbally frame it.

Recommended phrases to frame invisibility:

> *"Those with ill intent pass over me when they look."*
>
> *"Only those I wish to find me can see me."*
>
> *"Let spies see only blackened glass."*
>
> *"Let those who see/sense* (any image that pops in your mind) *instead."*

You can use these phrases as you grind a powder, light a candle, or perform a meditation.

About Invisibility Potion

Several years ago, one of my beginner witch books gave a recipe for an invisibility potion that called for vodka and poppy seeds. Since certain poppy seeds are used in heroin and opium production, the joke among my friends went something like "ingest that and you'll certainly *think* you're invisible!"

Since the book listed the recipe but no instructions, it was left to the reader to find someone willing to "share the secret" or experiment through ingestion (bad idea). It turns out the recipe did have some grounding in tradition: according to folkloric witchcraft, poppy seeds contribute to confusion (à la opium) and invisibility. The unseen part is attributed to tiny black seeds. A non-ingested version calls for placing shot glasses filled with vodka and poppy seeds in the corners of one's house where they are allowed to evaporate as a passive invisibility spell.

Additionally, invisibility has some grounding in baneful magick tradition. If you dig through old grimoires, many recommended poisonous herbs as a means of hiding from view. The clear benefit: if someone pokes at your defenses, they get sick. Nothing distracts quite as quickly as a sudden need to vomit. As someone experienced with metaphysical vomit (not mentioned in most modern witchcraft tomes), I encourage a milder approach to reduce collateral damage and save on steam cleaner rental costs.

Recipe: Invisibility Potion

The key to making an invisibility potion is the color black, as it is the absence of all colors. The noncolor makes it outstanding for invisibility as it is a non-light wavelength response to the light spectrum.[3]

Because of the non-light requirement, the safest, fastest, and most convenient choice for ingested invisibility potion? Coffee,

---

3. Jonathan Hogeback, "Are Black and White Colors?" *Encyclopedia Britannica*, accessed June 9, 2020, https://www.britannica.com/story/are-black-and -white-colors.

jet black. Though it's technically brown, it's black enough; also, brown is a color people tend not to notice. Have you ever heard someone mention beige as something that stood out?

YOU WILL NEED:
1 C ground coffee, any brand

1 pinch of black mustard seeds

1 t chicory root

3 crushed bay leaves

8 oz. water

Filter for brewing

This potion requires a coffee maker and a good quality filter. Pack your filter as tight as you can with ground coffee—fill it up. Add to this the black mustard seeds, a teaspoon of ground chicory root, and the bay leaves. Stir everything together, and explain your intention to the herbs. Describe how you wish this to manifest and, at the same time, name what and who you don't want to notice you. Make the coffee and allow it to cool. You can then use it one of two ways: (1) pour it in a bathtub full of water and soak in it or, (2) bottle it and add a tablespoon or so to your daily coffee for five days.

Recipe: Invisibility Powder
This powder works best for masking objects or small areas. To make powder residue less noticeable, use a cosmetic brush when dusting doors, windows, and miscellaneous objects. For storage, have a jar handy; an old prescription pill bottle also works fine.

YOU WILL NEED:

½ t dried fern spores or ground fern leaves

½ t poppy seeds

½ t Hawaiian black salt [4]

1 C corn starch

In an herb-dedicated coffee grinder or using a mortar and pestle, grind the fern roots, poppy seeds, and black salt until fine. Concentrate on your intentions as you work. When at a consistency that satisfies you, stir the mixture into corn starch. Mix as evenly as possible. Spoon the powder into your bottle or jar and label.

Domination

Some readers may remember certain witchcraft books of the 1970s that included spells of fascination and domination. These got labeled as "not nice" and cast aside when a new, ostensibly more moral witchcraft became popular. The Satanic Panic encouraged a wave of whitewashing witchcraft; all the energy for domination magick went instead to the marketing and advertising world.

I appreciate the idealism behind refusing this "not nice" practice. While I prefer to leave people to their inclinations, after enough intrusive, boundary-disrespecting nonsense, I also have come to understand the merits of intervention. After working in a shelter for women leaving domestic abuse situations, I believe this kind of idealism can lead to nonaction that can end in someone's

---

4 Hawaiian black salt is not the black salt of most witchcraft recipes. Black salt of traditional conjure and Craft is iodized salt infused with a cast iron pan's scrapings. The latter can aid invisibility work in an entirely different way, but it takes a little more energy to make this happen than it takes with Hawaiian salt.

death. There are people in the world, magickal or otherwise, who want what they want and use force to get it. They can't or won't care about the effect on those they take from. It takes a strong sense of self to accept that these people cannot be fixed, and it's just as true that you must sometimes fight off their manipulative evil for the sake of your survival.

Domination usually takes two forms: making yourself more likable to a person or group or immobilization. Most of the time, the sweetening strategy works best and comes with the fewest undesirable results. There are plenty of ways for it to be successful; in Conjure traditions, people use sweet jars. Burning pink candles or yellow ones with the name of the person you want to be nicer carved on the side or written in the glass with a marker encourages a gentler attitude towards you. Someone is far more likely to stop attacking you if they decide they like you rather than fear you.

Spell: Sweetening Your Sourpuss

Helping someone like you a little bit better can cut down on the need for defenses; after all, having genuine allies serves as one of the best defenses out there.

YOU WILL NEED:

One pink pillar candle

A knife to lightly carve the candle

1 tsp honey (to sweeten)

½ tsp sugar (to sweeten)

White carnations (optional, to purify)

A heatproof bowl

Prepare the candle by carving "(*Name of person*) is nice to me!" into it. Rub honey on the candle and then roll the candle in a half teaspoon of white sugar. Set it in the bowl and surround it with carnations if you choose to include them. If fire hazards are a concern, add about an inch of water to the bowl. Light the candle and allow it to burn for one hour each day, thinking of the person seeing you in a happy light. Chant/command the candle, saying, "See me in a better, sweeter light!" as you gaze at the candle for a few minutes each day.

Adjust the phrasing of the chant to suit your situation. Sugar, lavender, and sage can all clean up and sweeten the relationship between you and the other person. For situations with a lot of emotional baggage, you may want to use sunflowers or sunflower seeds to make the situation more optimistic while extracting poison between you. (Sunflowers were used in recovery of the soil after Chernobyl because they draw poisons out of the soil.) If you want to rectify emotions connected to financial issues, add a little mint.

Spell: Grinding Your Heel

If you want someone to stop something and niceties have failed, you need to apply pressure. A Conjure tradition calls for you to put a picture of your attacker's face down in your shoe. I have seen people work this effectively, with one caveat: the minute they remove the shoe, the person affected tends to go ballistic.

The following variation removes the need for shoes and reduces the risk of outbursts.

YOU WILL NEED:

A photo of the person

A jar with a lid

Pea-sized gravel/rocks

Black or purple candles (optional)

Bowl with water (optional)

Black or purple tea lights (optional)

Valerian and/or lavender (optional)

Place the photo face down at the bottom of the jar. Next, pour in the rocks, thinking of them as putting weight on and holding the person down until they calm down. If it feels right, speak the intention: "Until you calm, this pressure stays on you." After this, the only part of the self they can access is playing well with others. Add the valerian and lavender to keep the person calm. Close the lid tight. If desired, seal the working with wax by lighting the black and/or purple candle(s) and dripping the wax over the top of the jar. Place the jar in a bowl surrounded by water and burn black or purple tea lights on top of it. Store the jar in a dark place away from prying eyes. If you wish to break this spell, simply open the jar, empty the rocks, and burn the picture.

Confusion Spells

People that intentionally send bad energy tend to fixate. For whatever reason, they want your attention, your time, and usually a piece of you. The more time you spend fighting them, the more power they take from you, sapping the energy from your life. So if it's a response these people want from you, give them one! Just make the answer to their call so bizarre it causes a mental shutdown. For this purpose, we have confusion spells. I often add confusion elements to defensive workings. Bizarre occurrences, harmless but weird, are a great way to break someone's fixation.

My default strategy for adding confusion to spells is to reach into the proverbial herb bag, invariably starting with poppy seeds as they are affordable and reliable in confusion work. Black and yellow mustard seeds also help add to the disarray; for an added element of chaos, vinegar and red pepper can be included.

Recipe: Confusion Potion

This vinegar infusion makes a nice salad dressing or additive, so long as you don't charge it with intent. Since you probably will charge this, store it away from food—or then again, maybe you want things to get weird. However you entertain yourself is your business.

YOU WILL NEED:

A jar with a lid

1 T poppy seeds (to make things confusing)

1 T black mustard seeds (to hide things)

1 T yellow mustard seeds (to add an element of truth to the chaos, making it that much more confusing)

1 T dried red pepper (to heat the action)

Apple cider vinegar

Place the herbs in a glass jar with a cap or cork, layering the seeds on the bottom and peppers on top. Next, pour in vinegar to cover the herbs. Screw the lid on tight and store where sunlight illuminates the contents. The solar energy adds confusion; normally the sun reveals things but with this spell, it becomes part of blinding and obscuring. Daily, shake the container while imagining the most cartoonish and absurd situations you can. Do this for seven to nine days. Strain or leave the herbs in, as you desire.

Use an eyedropper and add a few drops to charm bags or dress the outside edges of candles (avoid rubbing your eyes afterward!). When using anything treated with this potion, wear gloves as a precaution. If you decide to leave a few drops where someone you want confused may cross, be very clear with the potion you want it to affect that person only.

Spell: Confuse Them into Leaving You Alone Spell

There's old folklore about goblins coming to the door and calling a person's name. To get them to leave, you had to answer with something that made no sense, for example "But the price of eggs in China is part of the color yellow!"

You can do this with people who use energy to gain access to your home or inner self to create chaos. By confusing them, they get too lost in their own world madness to bug you. It forces them to react rather than act.

YOU WILL NEED:

Chalk (any color)

Confusion potion (see above)

Something weird to say

Dip the chalk into your confusion potion. Draw a horizontal line on the floor at the entrance to your living space, crossing from one side of the door to the other. Imagine different energies trying to enter while chanting whatever bizarre thing comes to mind. Anyone metaphysically crossing your threshold without your consent will suddenly feel very confused about what's happening.

Spell: Run Devil Run

"Run Devil run" refers to a class of hoodoo spells meant to make a particularly nasty person skip town. To make this type of magick work, you need to find the part of yourself that can growl "Get out" Willow Rosenberg–style. When you're ready to run someone off, you almost always know who needs to leave. When you're trying to shove someone out to harm you and yours off your doorstep, you can't worry about where they land.

Before using this spell, I strongly suggest performing a domination spell to increase your odds of success. Domination compels the action you desire; using it to make a person hurting you or your family leave is absolutely an ethical application of this magick.

YOU WILL NEED:

A red candle and something to carve it with

A jar

A picture of the person you want to go

A pinch of sulfur (to take control of what bedevils you)

A little bit of ground walnut hull (to make it permanent)

A pinch of alum crystal (to stop any arguments dead)

A shoe, preferably one you don't wear often

Prepare the candle with banishing oil and the name of the person you want to banish. Carve their name down the side of the candle or write it on the glass with a marker.

Place the picture of the person causing trouble face down. Write the person's name on the back, and the words "Run from me NOW." Circle the image with the herbs. Take the shoe and hit the picture. Yell at it as though you wanted a wild animal out of your house. Scream at it, really let all your energy out on the "Run from me NOW!"

Once you have expended that energy, place the candle on top of the photo. Allow the candle to burn down completely. Feed the spell daily by beating the photo with your shoe. Continue until the person leaves for good. After the person leaves, put the picture, any candle wax, and other spell remnants in the jar. Hide it behind your toilet or on a designated "naughty" shelf (see page 92) where family members won't look for it.

In this chapter, the spells fall under the category of cursing or under "preparing to curse." When used properly, cursing is a tool of defense. When someone comes at you with violence, ideals must step aside to make room for reality. Match the energy and assert your right to exist … or watch your life be decimated.

Because people have more access to information about making magick work than ever before, it is necessary to expand the toolbox beyond "nice" and "approved" responses for security's sake. The problem with people who don't care about who they harm is that they don't care if *your* morals tell *you* to refrain from harming others. Moral high ground protects you from people who enjoy morality debates, not from the neighbor who peppersprayed your dog and threatened to do the same to your child.

For the people who need counter magick, the spells of this chapter offer a few ways to wrest back control of your life. I recommend doing some of these works in pairs of spells. For example, work invisibility alongside domination work. You could also cast a domination working with a reversal to really push back someone trying to overpower you. See what combinations work best for your situation.

NINE

HI, HERE'S YOUR BUTT BACK

Hex Twisting of So-Called Irreversible Spells

If you're alive, you can break any curse placed on you. Some may take years of work, therapy, self-healing, and self-awareness in addition to spirit work, especially any ancestral curse. But you can still remove every single one.

Some laws of the universe you can bend, but few if any can be broken. This is especially true when it comes to permanence: in this existence, the unchanging is not allowed. The laws of physics are the laws of nature. Nature always wins. People who attempt permanent curses are willfully ignoring this. Sure, energy can neither be created nor destroyed, but the matter must change. Our saving grace in all things? Entropy. The material world is constantly falling apart.

Curse breakings with proper fail-safes attached and unbindings can take hours or days to take effect. I could wrestle through these more direct approaches, or I could persuade a curse to curse itself. Because of this, I developed a time-saver technique inspired by a particularly effective incense recipe included in Herman Slater's *Magickal Formulary:* Hex twisting.

Twisting Spells Explained

A twisting spell takes extant negative energy and twists it back on the sender. Twists take more skill than reversal or mirror workings because you consciously catch the energy and reprogram it. You need to have a sense of energy flow, a skill that differs a great deal from traditional tool-based spellcasting. The methods vary depending on the style of magick that speaks to you most.

How to Capture and Bend Energy

For both folk work and the pure energy worker, two concepts/visuals must be understood: cords and intentions. While intention was covered a bit in the section on reversals, it's a nuanced topic. Intention crafting in and of itself is an intermediate skill in witchcraft.

Cords

Magick, trauma, and past life issues travel between people via energy cording. These cords effectively comprise a power grid, within which we experience our connection to other life, good and bad. The connections can include deities, spirits, and an array of other consciousnesses. Cords are often how bad and good energies come to us; all too often, and sometimes through no one's fault at all, these cords get tangled and toxic.

Some toxic cords leave easily with a simple cut and clear. Others take enormous emotional and spiritual work to detach. These cords create mutual vulnerability. Planting an attachment on one person exposes and possibly endangers the person who planted it. Yet we plant these cords intentionally and unintentionally all the time. Identifying and releasing these toxic cords is a necessary part of deep magickal work.

Spell: Knotwork/Cord Magick for Sealing Ties

Working exclusively with visualization practices can become difficult for longtime practitioners. Psychic attacks impair your concentration. Focus wavers less when you use physical objects that pantomime your desired outcome. Because of the interference, I created this spell so that it allows you to mimic unseen energy through physical touch. This way, you can make it work even with a limping attention span.

This spell allows you to grab a cord or cords attached to you from someone else and reverse the flow of energy. Think of it as an energetic backbend.

YOU WILL NEED:

Minimal distractions (you can perform this in a car with closed windows if you can't find an indoor space to be alone

A ball of string, twine, or thread

Scissors

Cut at least one string the length of your arm. Hold it between your hands and close your eyes. Scan your energy bodies, looking for threads that feel bad, off, or foreign. These cords, we are assuming, come from outside of yourself. You might sense groups of cords bundled together, wrapping together with attachments you want to have and some you don't want. Envision the string in your hand merging with one or all the cords that feel "off" within you. Once the cord in your hand resonates, feel for the tangles in your energy. Tie a knot in each end, forcefully saying, "I stop the flow!" Cut a new string and repeat this process for each off-feeling cord that you can identify.

Halting the energy works fine for most people. I like to add a second step to interrupt those who would reattach: Take one string and fold it in half. Knot the ends together. Next, twist it, fold it over itself, and twist again. Like the strong, the spell loops back to the originator, sending back what has been sent. The energy connects to them inside their energy bodies, creating a symbolic short-circuit in their soul's electrical system. If you feel especially angry, or if the person is notoriously violent and vindictive, you can hang the cord from a ceiling fan switched to the highest setting. If done well, this working causes enough confusion that whoever attached the cord to you will find themselves too busy to try again.

Hex Twisting with Energy

Many people who work with pure energy do so by instinct. Because they work almost entirely by intuition, they often struggle to teach their methods to others. I have some rudimentary skill at working solely with energy and now shall do my best to interpret my methods for your benefit. Based on my own experience,

I offer an imperfect description of how to handle cord work using felt/perceived energies rather than physical tools.

Seek the cord or cords tying you to the bad energy or situation and cut. Do this by imagining/feeling that cord and using an imaginary knife or pair of scissors. It helps if you make a noise that communicates the severance. If I imagine a cord between myself and another person, I might make a clicking noise with my tongue as I picture the scissors cutting the cord to reinforce to my subconscious that the cut has happened. There are complications to be mindful of: sometimes the cords involved are hidden, some are anchored to ideas and traumas we have internalized, and some are fakes planted as distractions. Worse still, extremely clever workers can place traps attached to these cords that cause larger problems if someone attempts to remove them. If your adversary is an advanced practitioner, you will benefit by using the caution level applied to defuse a bomb. Divine as thoroughly you can about those attachments.

Use a pendulum or have a friend coach you through a meditation to check your work and address any time bombs you might have been unable to spot during your work.

Break a Poppet Curse

If someone is serious enough to make a poppet of you, they're going to put a substantial amount of energy into it. Readings might tell you someone made a doll, but physical indicators tell you more. When someone has a doll of you that they torment, it often feels like mysterious aches and pains, or the sensation of a scratchy clothing tag rubbing your skin, except you can never find the tag. It can sometimes manifest as early flu symptoms that leave you exposed to the actual flu. If you know someone who practices Reiki, ask them to look closely at the energy flow. Some

Reiki healers can sense anything inorganic bound to your energy field. This ability isn't universal to all Reiki healers, so if the one you see can't, listen to what they do notice while working with your body. Keep in mind that after detection and healing on your own body, the poppet must still be addressed.

Effigies can be countered and switched off. Since the doll is of you, you have the important part that makes it work: your DNA and name. That's all you need to turn the doll around on the maker. You don't even need to know who made it.

Spell: Poppet Reversal Candle Spell

This spell turns the poppet of you into the poppet of whoever made it—making them their own worst enemy.

YOU WILL NEED:

One red and black glass jar reversal candle. If you can't get one, wrap the lower half of a red candle in aluminum foil.

Scissors

Reversal oil

A paper doll

Marker

String

Prepare your candle by poking holes in the wax and filling the holes with a reversal oil. The attitude to affect is "Nope, this mess is *yours.*"

On the paper doll, write the words "THE MAKER BECOMES THE MADE." I like this for the reflective quality of the language and the Mafia-esque tone. Take the poppet and tie it to the candle. I enjoy imagining strapping a cartoon character to a stick of dynamite as I do this. If your hands hurt from tying string, rubber bands serve just as well.

Light the candle and say, "Back atcha."

As the candle burns, it reverses the poppet connection to represent the person who made it instead of you.

Spell: Defeat Domination

As covered in chapter seven, domination spells attempt to control the behavior and choices of others. Domination and pressure workings demand subtlety; it can take serious self-awareness to catch when someone has put their thumb down on you!

Look closely at the areas of your life where you find yourself behaving strangely. Are you saying yes when you feel no? Do you know someone is disrespecting you, yet despite how you react to the same behavior in every other situation, you allow that disrespect to continue? To find where to cut the toxic thread, think about who might benefit from that strangeness. Once you identify that person, you can break free. This spell operates like a cut and clear but then seals off any vulnerability to someone pulling that string—or yanking that chain.

YOU WILL NEED:

String

Scissors

Tie a string around your wrist. Collect the energy of the spell placed on you and guide it to the string until the string vibrates at the same speed as the intruding energy. To find this resonance, imagine the spell as a layer over your emotional body. Picture the spell drifting out of you, as if it's a paper doll copy of you that transfers itself to the thread.

Say while using scissors to cut the string:

Snip and snap,

fall away

No more am I under this spell's sway.

Next, bind the spell to stop it from coming back again. Tie a knot as you say each number in the following rhyme. It is important to speak the words out loud for this spell, even if it feels silly. Bury the string or give it to a nearby stream or river.

With knot of one, the binding ties
now tie the one that had me tied

By knot of two, power over me is forever denied

With three, I turn this evil back:
attacks on me now them attack

At four, I tie their power source,
binding by time and by nature's force

At five, any try to control or
deny ends in nasty cracks

With six, the knot now breaks all links
and leads only to their own armor's chinks

By seven, the mere thought of me is
the source of a distracting jinx

At eight, I take my power back,
any given them I retract

Under nine victory is mine; what
they sent me they now attract

So Mote It Be!

Spell: Exploding a Curse

Blowing something up is both gratifying and dangerous. If you use this spell, make sure you perform it in a place where fireworks are legal. I highly recommend a large, empty parking lot with nothing to hit as the place to stage this magick. If you prefer not to draw attention to yourself, perform this at a fireworks-heavy holiday; no one will wonder what you're doing.

YOU WILL NEED:

A box, preferably cardboard, that fits over the firecracker (a shoebox with a lid is perfect)

Markers, pens, etc.

A firecracker

A lighter

A garden hose or gallon jugs of water for fire safety

Mark the box on the inside with your name, birth date, astrological information, and anything else someone might use to form a link to your energy. On the inside of the lid, write, "I break out of the hall of mirrors." Take the box outside, along with the firecracker and lighter. Light the fuse on the firecracker, quickly place the box lid on top, and stand back. This action makes a mess and obliterates the energy associated with any coffin box connected to you.

Hammer and Mirror

This is a practice most gratifying and dangerous. If someone puts you in a box, sometimes you must smash your way out. Wear goggles, gloves, long sleeves, and jeans for this. If you own steel-toed boots, wear them for this.

YOU WILL NEED:

A marker

A cheap mirror (you can buy these at craft stores)

A hammer

A shallow cardboard box

Goggles

A clean-up plan (dustpan and brush or broom, vacuum, etc.)

Long sleeves/protective clothing

Use the marker to write all your identifying information on the mirror. Put on goggles and heavy gloves. Place the mirror in the cardboard box. With one stroke, smash the mirror, imagining the mirror spells around your energy breaking. Place the cardboard box in a garbage bag, and be sure to sweep up any remaining glass shards that may have jumped out of the box. Discard the box and bag. If possible, also vacuum the area where you broke the glass.

Forwarding a Curse

Sometimes instead of fussing with the energy someone sends at me, I forward it. Like an email address shunting unwelcome messages to the recycling bin, this spell disperses energy I don't need or want. As described earlier in this book, depending on what someone sends me, I might "sell" their gifts to a spirit or contain them for future use. For instance, if someone sends a lot of fiery energy my way, I might ask the god Hephaestus if he wants that to power his forge. If I'm sent chaos in my direction, I might simply direct that energy to an abandoned toilet on a roadside somewhere. While you can forward this to specific individuals, always check with divination for the likelihood of unintended consequences.

Spell: Energy Redirect

If you don't care where the energy sent your way ends up, cast this spell.

YOU WILL NEED:

A piece of black construction paper

White chalk

A bowl and a vase

Your hair, picture, or something representative of you as bait

Set this spell up in any spot where you feel persistent intrusive energy in your home. On the construction paper, sketch a triangle. In the middle of the triangle, draw a circle. Imagine the circle as a black hole that vacuums all the junk in the room and sends it to a scrapyard dimension.

Set the vase in the center of the bowl. Drop in your hair or other personal effects. You may want to pour about a half-inch of water into the bowl to act as an additional trap for overflow energy. You can redirect the energy by drawing an arrow leading out of the circle and writing a word for where you want the energy to go. Popular choices include "up the sender's butt," "New Jersey Turnpike," and "Iowa."

I want to reemphasize at the close of this chapter: *there is no such thing as an unbreakable spell.* While psychic attacks can be persistent and nasty, they are never a permanent condition, no matter how hard someone may try to convince you otherwise. Additionally, you can't spend every minute of your waking life trying to identify a spell and how to break it. Sometimes grabbing the energy and adding a small distortion before sending it on will prevent someone from robbing you of time better used for inviting joy.

TEN

WHEN SPIRITS ARE JERKS

Handling Haunting, Harassment, and Hired-on Spirits

The unseen world contains multitudes. These beings, living entirely in the incorporeal, have their own cultures, perspectives, and laws. I would not describe the majority as hostile, nor would I ascribe them universal benevolence. The phrase "Wild Kingdom" applies to some, while "Byzantium" better describes others. Most of these beings mind their own business, but just like among humans, some need to make a living, and the work gets a little dirty.

There are many reasons a spirit might decide to harass you. Most commonly, someone hired it to give you some guff. On occasion, a spirit might be a natural predator. Empaths especially are prone to such hunting. Less frequently, you could find yourself dealing with a spirit you offended in a past life. Beings that live in a world of spirit instead of this three-dimensional one don't always experience time in the same way as humans. Things your great-grandparent forgot about remain current events to some of them. This can result in one version of multigenerational cursing.

While some spirit harassment situations are resolvable by invoking deities or more powerful spirits, or via rudimentary mediumship, even these methods can fail. Not all spirits want to negotiate, and some want a debt repaid no matter how outlandish the price. If you're new to practicing magic and offended a spirit, you need to seek outside help from experienced practitioners.

Signs of a Harassing Spirit

This list describes spiritual harassment/haunting but overlaps with general cursing.

- A general feeling of oppression
- Specific problem spots that seem to emanate a hostile mood
- Objects disappearing and reappearing
- Objects feeling "wrong" when you pick them up, with different textures and vibrations
- Electrical problems continuing after ruling out mechanical error
- Feeling a sense of something semisolid in empty spots
- Nightmares
- Inability to sleep because of persistent hypnagogic jerks
- Feelings of "not you" energies or cords winding in or through your body

- The disappearance of phenomena when you engage in sexual activity
- The disappearance of phenomena around salt
- The disappearance of phenomena around cast iron
- A powerful sense of anger ambient in your space after burning white sage

When these symptoms occur, perform a physical and spiritual cleansing. If you burn sage and the entity gets angrier, switch to a cleansing spray that includes black salt made in a cast iron pan. This mixture has touches of iron in it, which stops most but not all faeries dead in their tracks. If that does not quite work, add a few drops of colloidal silver to the spray. If this fails to stop the anger, use divination to identify the spirit.

The following list of substances can halt lower-grade spirit harassment. Incorporate these into your cleaning schedule or use them once every six months to give your home a spiritual tenancy turnover. Often the problem isn't a ferocious spirit so much as it is too many spirits passing through the home, creating chaos. A little whiskey on your walls may well end your troubles.

Banishing Spirits

Spirit banishers do what it sounds like—they make spirits nope out. Sometimes it's the vibrations of the material that drives them out. More often, it's the smell. When you use the following, always leave a door or window cracked—otherwise, the spirit just circles around in desperation to escape and becomes even more rambunctious. And take heed: some of these substances may make *you* eager to crawl out a window too.

Tibetan Spirit Purging Incense

Incense that has been prayed over 108 times by actual Tibetan monks, this variety smells nice and really can get rid of even some of the toughest of spirits. To date, I can only find two suppliers for this in the United States; there is no way to replicate this formula as it requires continuous prayer and preparation by Buddhist monks. (When searching for it online, use: "Tibetan ghost purging incense.")

Asafoetida and Arabic Black Salt

Demons hate the smell of these garlic-on-steroids seasonings. They don't want to be around them and will do the bare minimum on a contract and flee if these substances are anywhere near them. While this may still mean some demonic trouble for you if someone made a contract, it won't be thorough. You can purchase asafoetida at any Indian grocer, and most halal grocery stores carry black salt.

Sulfur

Sulfur does NOT get rid of demons. It will drive off faeries, ghosts, and other garden variety parasites. Demons *enjoy* sulfur/brimstone. However, wet sulfur effectively gets demons drunk. Only do this when you already know that a particular demon is a happy drunk.

Camphor

Camphor is a white, waxy substance extracted from the camphor tree. It may smell familiar to you, as it is often used in vapor rub formulas to treat chest colds externally. This substance clears out most (but not all) spirits of the dead. If someone has bound the spirit, camphor won't drive it off, but the spirit will be extra cranky. You can use this as leverage in negotiating a more stubborn spirit's departure.

Whiskey

Whiskey is a double-edged substance; it can block spirits and cleanse energy when applied externally but like all alcoholic beverages can also act as a signal that you consent to possession when ingested if not consumed with clear intention. Drawing a small, equilateral cross on each wall, the floor, the ceiling, and over each window can halt most random spirit traffic.

Communication

If the entity does not leave when using baseline eviction products, you need to identify it and find out what it needs to leave. You may have to choose between negotiation and exorcism. In some cases, the spirit may want to leave but be unable to due to a contract or binding.

Spirit communication is the most efficient way to deal with a misbehaving spirit, but it is not always the easiest. It takes a certain skill set to ask directly what the hell it's doing and take a moment to listen, because spirit communication often requires clairaudience. Although clairaudience may develop over time with practice, you don't have time to wait for it evolve if you haven't slept in three weeks because a spirit is harassing you. Seek outside tools to interact with the spirit. While a reliable medium is probably the best help in this situation, spiritual clairvoyants are not always accessible or affordable. Pendulums can work for a conversation but have limits. When you're stuck in your situation, you need to devise your own means of communication ... or suck up your superstitions and use a spirit board.

Settle yourself near where you feel the spirit most. If you cannot have an open conversation in that space, close your eyes and picture it. I often invite the spirit to sit down at my kitchen table. I put out a glass of water, whiskey if it feels necessary, and possibly a little bit of food. Once settled, I pose questions and wait for a response.

I have found that the single best question to ask is "What's going on?" The next best for follow up is "So what do you need?" Read the emotional timbre of the energy you receive. While some spirits speak your language/use words, many use images or show you references familiar to themselves that may not translate to what you know. More practiced spirits may show you images from television shows they've see you watching or music they've heard you listen to. Be patient. Make sure you understand as best as possible what they're asking, and be honest if you do not fully understand. Do not make any promises to the spirit, especially not in the first communications. Understand fully what it needs and wants, and be firm about what you can and cannot give.

Negotiating with a Spirit Hired to Harass You

Often, especially persistent spirits are hired by other magick workers. The reasons for doing so are as myriad as human social and psychological dysfunctions. Most of these spirits have their own motivations for taking the job. The payment allows them to exist in the material world and gives them something to do if they find the spirit world boring or troublesome. Except in extreme cases where what's harassing you is already personal to the spirit, most entities allow you to buy out their contracts.

Contract buyouts require different things, depending on the spirit. Blood is certainly an option but never the only choice. Often a spirit will request something unique to your talents that also serves their interests. Over the years, I have made herbal balms, written poetry on sidewalks, and cast specific spells on behalf of these spirits in exchange for dissolving contracts on me. Others were happy to quit the old contract in exchange for a shot of whiskey and a shiny penny. It all depends on what they get from working on you in the first place. If they dislike the person that initially hired them, this can also aid your relationship and allow for a very lenient negotiation. There is only one absolute rule in spirit negotiations: only make promises you can keep— spirits have long memories and absolutely will come to collect. Keep in mind that you may not have any luck getting the name of the spirit's sender. Spirits generally keep their client confidentiality sacrosanct unless the laws of hospitality were violated (very annoying when you want to know who is attacking you).

Working with Spirits for Protection

If you get as far as negotiating with a spirit that has been harassing you, you may have the option of hiring them to protect you. After all, they have the qualities you need: they know exactly what's getting thrown at you and how to stop it. This practice does require agreeing to a payment schedule. You can pay a spirit by burning ancestor money (universally accepted in the world of spirit) or by building altars, playing music that the spirit prefers, or engaging in a wide variety of activities that give the spirit something it needs to have an environment conducive to its work. A schedule may involve a daily or weekly payment, and some spirits prefer to set schedules according to their preferred moon phases. In situations with more than one spirit in your house, ask them to name a foreperson. A point of contact always aids group projects.

Spirit Identification

Figuring out what spirit you're working with and what it needs requires a process of identification. While many people intuitively know what spirit it is, it's an ability few people are born with. Also, spirits rarely manifest in ways popularized in fiction. For example, few fairies bear any resemblance to their popular representation; think less Disney and more Grimm.

Demon Hauntings

If a demon harasses you, it's far more noticeable than interference from other spiritual entities. Most readers spent their formative years defining good and evil by nature rather than action and were exposed to many stories painting demons as evil for evil's sake. You certainly won't agree with the idea that demons are not evil while dealing with a diabolic haunting. Yet of all the entities in the spirit world, demons are the most willing to communicate and the most respectful about boundary setting...once certain cultural expectations were met. Demons are not inherently evil. Just like other spirits, they sometimes take jobs to fulfill their own needs. They do, however, enjoy the hell out of their reputations.

Most information about warning signs of demonic attacks comes from people who have experience with Goetic beings. Demons from other cultures share some of the same hallmarks but often execute mischief in a very different way. Information in English on this is not easily available; if you determine that the demon comes from an outside culture, try to find someone from that culture who can help you understand its behavior and needs. Each demon has its values, agendas, and morality. Some demons also have a greater sense of subtlety than others. While the following list can indicate a demonic attack, you can experience one without any obvious symptoms. These obvious symptoms only happen when they benefit from you knowing a demon is doing the haunting.

SIGNS OF DEMONIC HAUNTING

- The smell of sulfur/rotten eggs

- A feeling of an oppressive presence

- The physical sensation of bumping into someone/feeling a solid presence even though, visually, you see nothing

- Psychokinetic incidents often associated with poltergeists: objects moving on their own, doors slamming, and localized weather phenomenon

- Clear voices in your mind that you know aren't yours[5]

- The feeling of physical impact with no visible cause

- Marks on your skin after nightmares, such as hand marks, scratches, and bites

- Common energy cleansers like sage, palo santo, and camphor fail to remove the smell/feel

Be aware that there are several signs of demonic haunting that are also signs you own a cat. Your cat may also be a demon, but you signed up for that, so perhaps look at this as an added chapter in your pet care guide. Additional overlapping signs include strange sounds made at night, mysterious dead animals on your doorstep, and time and space bending solely because someone somewhere is hungry.

There is a civilized way to end or reduce most demonic hauntings, but it takes nerves of steel and calming your prejudices. That

---

5. An ability shared with angels.

method? Give the demon the same courtesy and hospitality you offer a neighbor with whom you share a fence.

When I find a demon causing me trouble, I invoke the laws of hospitality, set out some whiskey and the spiciest beef jerky I can find, and invite them to have a chat. It is often helpful to ask for a name or use a demon deck to identify and read up on the demon if your clairaudience or clairvoyance is weak. Knowing the name will not, as rumored, give you complete power over the being. However, the name can help you find other practitioners online who have worked with the entity and discovered what offerings it likes. Considerate behavior helps you entice it to make a contract with you instead of the original sender.

Demons are mercenaries and business brokers, first and foremost. Generally, as the conversation progresses, the demon will ask for something ridiculous and offensive. It usually does not want this; it wants to see your reaction. When it makes this request, give it a counteroffer, and explain why: "I *would* give you pig's blood, but I'm vegan. Is there a particular type of red wine you enjoy?" Eventually, you will come to a compromise.

Note: Offerings of chocolate are almost universally applicable in the spirit world. Oddly, sugar is not, although it goes a long way with many. Keep dark and milk chocolate on hand if a lot of spirit activity happens in your home. Fairies and demons often compromise (at least temporarily) for good quality chocolate.

Faery Hauntings

Most hauntings with physical phenomena such as moving objects, rearranged items, and mysterious scratches trace back to a faery as the culprit. Even the most humanlike of them are wild compared to humanity (no matter how feral the human); in their minds, it's their way of living that is the "right" one, not the human way. No authority spiritually regulates the Fae; they are equal to humans in sentience and sometimes go to war based on their belief systems.

The Fae are tricky to identify and work with because the most incontrovertible laws of nature bind them in addition to the laws of faery society. Time moves slower for them, making them both prone to fickleness and fixation. Most do not distinguish your present self from any past life version of you. Because of their longevity, they can hold grudges over something an ancestor you resemble stole. Said faery might also be mad because of where you stepped, where you threw your trash, or because they heard you say something disparaging about the Fae.

SIGNS OF A FAERY HAUNTING

- Not only does sage cleansing not work, it also angers the spirit.

- A persistent sense of chaos reigns through the house.

- You can never find *anything* you're looking for.

- Marks and scratches on the skin upon waking up.

- Faeries may try to drag you from your bed; you will feel a tugging on your limbs. Some might even succeed and may count pulling a blanket off you as a partial success.

- Guests having moments of behaving like they're drunk despite no ingestion of alcohol or other substance.

- Items disappearing and reappearing in threshold spaces, e.g., balanced over doorways, on top of curtain rods, and between window glass and screen.

- Despite the faery having bad intentions, often the energy feels very "white light."

- Conversely, certain fairies will instead feel palpably malevolent but show up to help.

Like demons, faeries can possess people. The difference is that demons do so with explicit consent; the Fae operate on implied consent. In other words, a faery will get you to say yes without realizing what you are saying yes to. Fae possession tends to come with much more chaotic energy, hysterical laughter, fear of metals, and sometimes a need to destroy mass-produced objects.

While sometimes faeries accept payment to harass someone, their motivation is almost always personal. If a faery accepts a job, they are simply accepting payment for something that they already want to do. Usually, they do as they do out of jealousy because someone violated a natural space or because they're ill. Regardless of the situation, you're going to need to put in some work to resolve an issue.

The most efficient way to get a faery to calm down is to put out some whiskey with whole-fat cream in it, either at your doorstep or in a hearth space. Tell the faery you're sorry and leave it out for twenty-four hours. At the end of the twenty-four hours, put down a piece of chocolate and say, "I'm listening." Then sit and listen, making sure you have absolutely no distractions, especially not an electronic distraction. Sometimes the faery will tell you what you did wrong. It may speak in words or project images into your mind. Most of the time, it's resolvable, and there's something you can do. It may ask you to bring a land offering somewhere, make medicine, or put something back that you took. The only time I could not resolve a dispute was when one particular faery was convinced that I stole her boyfriend. Telling her that I didn't want her boyfriend did not help. I settled it by appealing to her faery court for judgment and intervention. To my relief, they wanted her to knock off her bad behavior, too. Last I checked, she is still in time-out.

Acts of appeasement should cause the poltergeist-like activity to subside. If it does not, you will need some traditional witch's black salt or iron powder if you can get a hold of it. Put the black salt or iron powder around all the thresholds of windows, doors, and closets. If the fairies cling and continue to cause trouble, Christian prayers combined with faery incense should help. The Fae inherently dislike the trappings of Christianity for the same reason the colonized always dislike the colonizers.

Djinn Hauntings
No djinn haunts anyone "just for fun." Most of these entities only harass other beings when forced to do so; if you have an enemy willing and able to summon djinn, you need to put a microscope to all of your relationships. When someone sends a djinn to you, it's already cranky because it doesn't want to be there. And if you come from a culture outside the Middle East, you have to deal with the realities of intercultural exchange to resolve such a haunting. Suppose you're not from a culture that acknowledges djinn and you want to avoid cultural appropriation during a djinn haunting. If you attempt such a way, it's going to fail. Western methods don't budge djinn. Unless you actually address the djinn in rituals they understand and respect, you're going to be stuck with very angry, supremely powerful spirits for a very, very long time. Be prepared for them to give you nightmares, beat you up at night, and cause massive issues in every area of your life.

While the power of Christ doesn't compel djinn, hospitality does. Most djinn practice Islamic faith and culture, with the exception of a few determined Pagans.[6] They will disappear temporarily for events they consider "dirty" (such as sex) but reassert themselves and punish you later for actions they perceive as *haram* (unclean). These attacks are not personal—the djinn are acting on the rules of their culture as they know them. As far as they are concerned, you are subject to those rules no matter who raised you.

SIGNS OF A DJINN HAUNTING

In general, nearly anything you would see from a demon haunting, you will see here, except there won't be any reaction to holy water or Christian symbols. In addition are the following:

- Hearing chanting/muttering, especially in shadowy corners of the home
- Dogs reacting to invisible harassment
- A general mood of wrath after ingesting alcohol or consuming pork products (this does not always happen; it appears to be a matter of personal-to-the-djinn opinion)
- Frequent nightmares featuring an entity with glowing red eyes
- In some (but not all cases, the scent of garbage/landfill

The most efficient way to stop a djinn attack is to assume an attitude of kindness and hospitality. If you have strong negative feelings about Middle Eastern and South Asian cultures, find someone who thinks differently than you to help you with this. If you bring in your prejudices, you will make your problems worse.

---

6. "Paganism" to a djinn means pre-Islamic folk religions, a very different set of faith practices from Neopaganism.

Djinn recognize truth and sincerity. They are also sensitive about bigotry toward themselves.

If you believe you have a djinn haunting, set out a plate of dried fruit. These spirits appreciate figs, dates, and apricot ears, along with some mint or rose petal tea. Out loud, thank them for their visit and honor them as guests. Walk through your house, opening each door and window one at a time as you play the Muslim call to prayer over speakers or your phone. Emote an attitude of "come and pray" as you do this. When I performed such a banishing, the djinn thanked me for my hospitality as they departed. The kinder ones forcibly collected any hostile members who attempted to linger.

Ghost Hauntings

Ghosts, for the sake of this book, are limited in scope to departed human spirits. While the reasons/cause of the haunting vary by personal history, they can revisit as angry/injured ancestors. In some cases, people did not factor in that free will continues upon death; these are spirits just waiting around for some direction as to what to do next. Often, to remove or relocate a ghost you don't need the story, but sometimes you do. Your best bet to find out which approach to take is to perform divination or get a reading from a professional experienced in working with the dead.

SIGNS OF A GHOST HAUNTING
- Concentrated cold spots in areas with no drafts
- Human-personality smells, such as perfumes, cooking smells, and the like, with no traceable source
- Hearing footsteps in an otherwise still house

- An awareness of a person taking up space, with no visible person nearby

After dealing with angry mercenary demons, fairies, djinn, astral projections, and the occasionally pissed off deity, a good old-fashioned haunting by a dead spirit delights me. Even violent dead spirits are manageable once you understand them. Primarily, it's about having firm boundaries and being willing to hold your elders accountable for their actions in a reasonable way. The difficult part comes when you must account for how hauntings cross over your traumas and prejudices.

Identifying a ghost takes little effort. Dead spirits have the temperature of the grave. They are not automatically hostile, but your lizard brain (if unaccustomed to the paranormal) may disagree. Only by remaining calm and grounded can you discern what's happening with a haunting. The vast majority of hauntings can be resolved with polite conversation about conduct and etiquette in your home. You won't know if you need banishing methods until you give the ghost a chance to cooperate.

If you work with your ancestors or have spiritual problems with ancestors, you will need to approach things differently from how you would a random haunting if a dead relative is the source of your discomfort. It's always harder to set boundaries with family, even when they're dead. If you know the ghost to be an ancestor, I encourage you to research ancestor work. A growing body of healers is teaching how to deal with these trauma issues.

Ghosts usually appear because of their own needs, although some do haunt for hire. Some just want a place to hang out. Others might have unresolved trauma. A specific cross section discovers that moving into the light is optional and decide to stay there. Pay attention to those voluntary types—they're the ones who can make real trouble. Ghosts that take jobs are dangerous and know how to dodge most banishment techniques. The especially clever outsource, choosing to hire spirits that are not ghosts to do their work and make sure it sticks. This way, their hapless target never can figure out what storm they stand in. The most efficient way to find out if someone hired a ghost to haunt you is to get a reading and then see if the ghost did any outsourcing. Look for coin and sword suits crossing each other with the Moon card or Death inverted somewhere in the mass. You will need to clear away whatever the clever bastard came up with before banishing the spirit. Clearing the ghost itself will still work once you identify it, although you might want to have a friend help you with it, to raise energy behind your intention.

Most of the time, all you need to do to remove a ghost is burn a little bit of prairie or common sage and open a door or window. That's it. Tell the sage you want the ghost to go somewhere else, naming a specific location, and there it goes. Popular choices include different planets, the ocean, and the basements of various corporations. In some cases, if you know the correct afterlife location, you can invite the deities of that culture to come collect. If you hate the smell of sage, use rosemary. You can also place crumbled camphor in the corners of rooms in which you encountered the ghost. Make sure you seal your home against further intrusion by burning frankincense or copal incense at the doors and windows when finished. Leaving an offering to a chthonic (deep earth/death) deity with a request to prevent all hauntings can also help.

If a ghost is feeding on living energy to stick around on the material plane, it usually has compulsive behaviors it likely also had while alive. You will know if it does because someone in your house will feel tired all the time for no discernible reason or may have episodes of sleep paralysis. You may find flickering lights, as ghosts can tap into and drain electric objects such as light bulbs and batteries. You may sometimes feel the sensation of invisible teeth sinking into you. If a ghost was a psychic vampire in life, it will continue the feeding behavior in death.

Working: Evicting a Ghost

To handle more compulsive dead humans, use noise and bossiness to evict. Ring a bell to command attention and then, in a strong voice, give the spirit a job to do that will take a long time to complete. I usually demand that these spirits count every grain of sand, every star in the sky, and every drop of water in the ocean. Some practitioners believe they may somehow finish the jobs and return to you in future lifetimes. When that happens, all it takes is coming up with a new job for the ghost or asking them to check one another's work. Most hauntings are benign. In most situations, informing the ghost of house rules calms them down or persuades them to exit. Because these were once living entities, you have to frame your boundaries a certain way as some are sensitive about their existential status. On occasion, a ghost gets stubborn and requires a specific direction or compulsion. Often, the ghost needs grief counseling.

In the case of violent hauntings, always walk through the process for benign ghosts first. Sometimes ghosts get angry and seem like a problem, but when approached civilly, they behave better; sometimes the violent outburst comes from an attempt to protect you. Certain human spirits eventually become evil in life or death and get labeled demons because of the harm they did in life. While ideals you have may tempt you to expend effort in healing them, think about what performing that sort of healing is about for you. Dead or alive, the emotionally damaged must ultimately fix themselves. That process starts by seeking appropriate avenues of healing while upholding respectful boundaries. The most efficient way to end a violent haunting is to pray to spirit, play drum and rattle music, and burn spirit purging incense, all at the same time. If the spirit resists even that, playing Bobby McFerrin's "Don't Worry, Be Happy" on repeat causes even the most violent entities to vacate. If you opt for McFerrin, remove anything breakable from the haunted space beforehand.

Negotiating with Big Bads

When I talk about "Big Bads," I'm speaking of scary beings, ones that do not like you, ones that always have trouble in mind and the kind of power that just might squish you; ones with recognizable names like Beelzebub, Baba Yaga, or Set.

Here's what I have to say about these Big Bads: Yes, most of them are scary. They are not playing by polite society's rules, especially not any perceived rules about good or evil. They have a part to play in this universe, in its balance, and the spiritual development of humanity. I won't say they're here to teach you, but you *will* end up learning. They aren't generally benign, but they also have bigger fish to fry than you.

These beings are not, in any sense, the mosquitoes of the spiritual ecosystem. Like most apex predators, they keep an important balance in this world. If you encounter them, it's either because you did something to get their attention or someone else directed their attention to you. If all the world's a stage, there's still a much bigger play happening, bigger than the earth and sky and stars. Nobody outside your plotline is watching your story.

The reason I bring up the Big Bads is not that you will need to defend against them. I bring them up because many lesser spirits will try to convince you that they are those beings to increase your fear. The number of female-identified demons that call themselves Lilith are legion, but there is only *one* Lilith. And that Lilith has zero interest in causing sleep paralysis or sending men naughty dreams. However, some lesser demons love to puff themselves up, thinking it will put you at a disadvantage.

If you find yourself facing one of these major entities and know without a doubt that's who you met, here's what you need to know: they are there because you have something they want that only you can do. Never assume you are special because of this. You just happen to fall into a certain place or time, and the more you cultivate your humility, the more you will know exactly where you stand.

You can say no to any being, ever. You always have a choice. You have every right to ask for a need to be met in exchange for your service.

Always begin negotiation from a place of civility. Find out what offerings they like, set out what you consider reasonable. If you're unsure, offer a glass of water. Rice and potatoes also appear universally acceptable, especially if you add hot sauce. Just because everyone says something is evil doesn't mean it is. Those who went through the high school experience know how rumors and common knowledge can be nothing more than lies. Some entities are as good-hearted as any white light being out there, and they still might make your skin crawl. The more you learn to sit with discomfort, the better you can master spirit interactions, especially when you move up the power scale.

Always have a counteroffer ready. If someone wants forty swine, counteroffer with a plate of bacon. Establish deadlines and keep to them. Emphasize the year of delivery in the agreed-to deadline. Always think very carefully about what you request from that spirit and how that spirit may interpret that request. While you may want wealth, if the entity comes from a culture that measures wealth in property, you might find a cow in your office. Also, make sure you structure leaving you alone as part of the contract when the exchange of services complete.

Trapping Large Spirits

If all negotiations fail and your ability to live your life is continuously affected, you may need to resort to large scale spirit trapping, which differs greatly in risk from the method in chapter five. To do this safely, hire an experienced shaman or spirit worker. Spirit trapping is, unfortunately, not an affordable service for most people. The worker risks possession, physical injury, and attacks from the spirit in question. I have had extremely competent spirit workers come back to me, requesting hazard pay after situations escalated. If it's bad enough that you need it and you have exhausted all other options, be ready to pay for the help.

If you can't afford a professional to assist, you have one other option: you can hire a spirit to do this work. Often the spirits most amenable to this are demons. Demons live halfway between the world of the corporeal and the world of spirit, making them ideal for putting a stop to aggressive spiritual attacks. The catch is that demons (and sometimes angels) require payment. The fee agreed upon is between you and that demon and will usually involve demonstrating skill or trade on your part. And if you cut such a deal, *never* renege on your payment. Any spirit will harass you for that. The entire world operates on energy exchange. If you make a promise, give your due. Failing that, you can try building your spirit trap.

Working: Large-Scale Spirit Trap

I developed this larger spirit trap under the tutelage of the Goetic demon Belial. Yes, I did agree to give him credit. It can serve as a general trap, and the choice of hiring a spirit to ensure the correct entity ends up in it is your decision to make.

YOU WILL NEED:

A large bottle, preferably a blue wine bottle (blue draws spirits and the light diffusion from this color confuses them once they crawl in the bottle)

A tiny pair of scissors

Superglue

A shoebox to set the bottle in, upright

Netting (such as what you might cut from a bag of oranges or onions, or burlap)

Sewing pins

Pieces of your DNA (hair works fine)

A magnet or receptive lodestone that fits inside the bottle

Honey or sugar

Black ink

Olive oil or molasses (optional)

A cork

Sealing wax and a lighter

Wash the bottle and allow it to dry. Superglue a pair of scissors, pointing upwards, at the neck of the bottle. They cut the spirit's ties to any controllers. Set the bottle in the box. Place the net around the bottle's neck so that the mouth remains open, and the material rests on the "shoulders" of the glass. Pin the edges of the fabric from your net to the inside of the shoebox. The net doesn't trap the spirit per se; it catches any residual energies or lesser spirits accompanying the larger troublemaker. Drop the lodestone and your DNA inside the bottle. Add honey or sugar and some black ink. If you want more material for the entity to "swim" through or get stuck in, you can fill the bottle more, adding a little bit of olive oil or molasses.

Place the bottle in a spot you and your hired spirit, if you employed one, agreed to. The spirit will finagle the pest into the bottle and inform you, in the manner you agreed upon prior, when it's there. The spirit will be trapped in the oil, giving you time to cork and seal the bottle. To dispose of the trap, you can take this bottle to a river and send it downstream. If the possibility of water pollution bothers you, bury it away from your property, preferably in a cemetery where you have spent time cleaning abandoned graves and bringing offerings to the dead. If pressed for time, space, or transportation, I often use a public garbage can at a city intersection or garage to dump my spirit traps. In my mind, leaving them in a public garage is still leaving the spirit at a crossroads because several vehicles meet, pause, and disperse there. If you're worried about the bottle breaking and the spirit getting out, name the trap as an offering to the Roman deity Cloacina. Cloacina, the goddess of gutters, takes offerings from garbage and sewers. Once Cloacina claims something, there's no escape!

DIY Exorcism or Hiring an Expert

Exorcism is not the complex ritual most people think it is. Anyone who practices space clearing performs a rite of exorcism, made so when something fights clearing out during a routine house cleansing. It is generally easier than spirit trapping. You don't need to cut a deal, build any traps, or employ any trickery. For most exorcisms, all you need is your *I Mean It* (also known as "Mom") voice and a specific somewhere else to go. In some situations, you may need a specific someone to take your haunting buddies somewhere else but, ultimately, the point of exorcism is eviction and relocation. People balk at the word "exorcism" because of publicity in mainstream culture, mostly from movies such as *The Exorcist*. Certain churches make rites of exorcism mysterious or even heretical. Many people therefore think the spiritual version of yelling "Get your butt outta my house!" is a complex and dangerous operation. It's not—it just sounds cooler in Latin. Yelling "get out!" usually works.

Although rare, it sometimes happens that you might need more than "I mean it" and an expelling herb smoldering in your oven-mitted hand. Complex exorcisms that require a big ritual happen when dealing with a hired spirit that believes you reneged on an agreement or when you move into a home inhabited by a spirit that thinks you're the one invading its house. What prompts a spirit to relocate depends upon the spirit; because of this, there is no universally applicable general exorcism ritual.

Whatever structure you use to perform such a rite, it needs to have the following elements:

- An identification of the spirit causing trouble.
- An offering of food and drink, presented by you in good faith.
- A means by which the spirit may communicate with you.

- If you feel it necessary, a protector spirit or intercessor such as a death deity, angel, or demon. Only call on spirits with which you have an established relationship.

- A place for the spirit to go to, preferably one where any land spirits have already consented to receive said spirit.

- Carefully planned and crafted language about where the spirit needs to go, when it should leave, what it should take with it, and under what (if any) circumstances it may return.

All exorcisms benefit from the above parameters. Beyond that, the specific offerings, communication, and relocation all depend on the spirit. For example, removing a fae often requires finding out what its original habitat looked like. Demons tend to look forward to going to hell if you frame it well—most that require exorcism only hang out because someone who called them up for a job tried not to pay, or you happen to be the job. Angels usually require intervention from an archangel or a demonstration of the truth of a matter.

If the entity poses too much danger and is unwilling to communicate, move on to spirit trapping. A caveat: Many people tend to forget that lands and waters have a consciousness as well. Exorcism, banishing, and spirit trapping does not work on animistic spirits—the spirit of a mountain isn't going to relocate, and it's not about to climb into a bottle. Often when animistic spirit hauntings occur, it's because you damaged something or you took something away from its home. If this is where your spirit activity issues are rooted, make an offering of water to the land you live on, and take inventory of any items you recently removed from their natural habitat. You may need to return something, create medicine, or make some other amends.

The Difference between Exorcism and Spirit Trapping

When you trap a spirit, you're going to the trouble of building a jail and disposing of the spirit later. I consider spirit trapping a final resort after attempting exorcism but prioritized it first because some people picking up this book have already landed in a situation well past the point of a polite renegotiation of location. In some situations, spirit trapping functions as an execution, so performing it has more potential consequences than a simple relocation/exorcism practice. It is best reserved for spiritual activity that causes genuine psychological and physical harm. What follows is an exaggerated example, but a good guideline: if a spirit behaves in any way that the demon in the movie *Paranormal Activity* does, skip the exorcism and go for the trap.

Banishment

The idea behind banishment is "you don't have to go home, but you can't stay here." The spirit worker conjures energy that just encourages an intruding spirit to leave. Often this practice takes relatively little energy to perform, in part because the "don't want" feeling for many of us comes from a primal place within that also reacts when we encounter smells we dislike. Some magick practitioners have the opinion that banishment is preferable to exorcism. I acknowledge the reasoning behind this idea; banishing doesn't harm anything, and it doesn't infringe on free will. All it does is establish a boundary that says, "OK, you can exist, just not here."

While banishing proves useful in some cases—especially on living beings you want out of your place of business immediately, for example—I find that this approach often has more unintended consequences than exorcism or spirit trapping. When you banish something with "OK but not here," the spirit must still find somewhere else to go. So, if you simply banish a spirit from your bedroom, it may turn and hang out in the kitchen or living room. If you show it the door to your apartment building, it may terrorize psychically sensitive people staggering home at the end of their third-shift jobs. Banish too often without enough direction to the banished spirits, and there goes your neighborhood. Because I have seen banishings create unintended chaos this way, I try to reserve that clearing/energy technique for situations involving live human beings who, in most situations, really do already have somewhere else to go.

Exorcism for an Unknown Spirit

If you never identify a spirit to tailor the exorcism to its nature, try this energy work method. You may also want to use this when you know the spirit type, as a means of preparation for that working. Ground yourself with intensity. Put time and, if possible, physical weight into it. If you can, lie under a weighted blanket while meditating. Feel the Earth's gravity in your feet. Work yourself into the most entitled, demanding mindset possible because you are about to wage a territory battle and must stake your claim.

Take deep breaths into your belly. Imagine the inhalations filling your root, sacral, and solar plexus chakras. Get those energy points spinning. Select a place for the spirit to go. Choose a location hard to return from. Designate an activity for the spirit when it arrives at your chosen destination. If you want it in the fires of hell, say so, also telling it to work the sulfur mines. Send it to a fictional planet, an ice floe, or a forgotten cave at the bottom of the sea. If it has fire alignments, direct it to the corona of the sun. Give the spirit these instructions with gusto. Announce this and open a window or a door. Despite spirits not physically needing them, they still use them.

If you want to raise energy to back your territory claim, chant a litany. If you wish, you can use something directly from Catholicism. A priest might tell you it's only to be used by a priest. Even today, traditional religio-patriarchal authorities claim authority over things they have no business controlling. Exorcism happens to be one of those things. If you're around anyone who starts lecturing you about how you'll go to hell for protecting your family and yourself spiritually, feel free to say, "OK, patriarch," and move on. It is always good and right to protect yourself spiritually and physically; you need no permission to do so.

If you feel any fear or menace as you speak, invoke backup. Archangel Michael helps in exorcisms regularly. Make sure you say thank you to him after the rite finishes. He doesn't necessarily need a prayer litany but candles are nice.

If you need words more complex than "get the hell out" and don't have a religious tradition, you can always create your own or use this sample:

> *I command and compel you,*
> *Out—to the ocean, to the sea*
> *To the endless salt and wash*
> *Go there. Be.*
> *This house refuses you;*
> *My spirit rejects you*
> *By the power of land and sky*
> *By the power of heaven on high*
> *By the power of death and life—*
> *LEAVE MY HOUSE.*

When the spirit leaves, you will feel a lifting of the atmosphere, like a sense of reduced physical pressure. Chant "leave" with any swear words you like while burning a spirit banishing incense for a strong effect. Seal your work with a resin incense such as frankincense.

In most situations, only full-time magicians deal with the range of entities mentioned in this chapter. This work can become quite complicated, especially for those with profoundly mixed ancestries and spiritual legacies. If you find yourself having repeated unsolicited dustups with spirits, reach out for help. Whether it's an especially determined spiritual attack, a past life/ancestral intersection issue, or payment for some crime committed, something larger is going on. Many of us have been shamed into silence for having spiritual struggles at all. There is help for this so long as you are willing to adapt your worldview enough to allow the assistance to work. I know. It's hard.

ELEVEN

THAT WAS TERRIBLE, LET'S NOT DO THAT AGAIN

Recovery and Prevention after Spiritual Trauma

Clearing a spiritual attack may be the denouement of a story in your life, but it's not the conclusion of the episode as far as your emotions may be concerned. Afterward, you're going to need spiritual and possibly medical care—and that absolutely includes mental health assistance. Metaphysical injuries also translate to the physical, so if something hurts, get it checked. For example, a friend of mine visited a chiropractor after an encounter with a psychic vampire. She found that her hips misaligned with her spine so severely that the doctor couldn't figure out how it had happened!

But there's more to recovery from a cursing than just restoring the body. Magickal attacks can throw aspects of your life out of alignment. Money, timing, and relationships can all need repair. You also must respect any trauma responses you developed: emotional experiences are real, which means emotional injuries are also real. Much of magickal energy affects real places we commonly perceive through imagination. Given the nonmaterial nature of magick, once such an attack ends, we question our sanity.

It's normal to wonder if the whole thing happened or if your brain conjured it from some dark, awful, and deeply inconvenient recess. After all, only some of these attacks leave physical scars on the body. Those that appear often disappear after we overtake the source of the attack; although forgetting it happened may be comforting, the disappearance of a noticeable mark can also add to our cognitive dissonance over an energetic attack happening at all. But unlike scars, trauma often does not just naturally resolve itself. To recover from it, we need to retrain our brains to leave fight/flight mode to return to clarity.

Why "Don't Tick People Off" Is Bad Advice

A helpful demon once suggested that I not make people angry so often. Demons are wonderful and wise beings, but they are not omniscient—their emotional intelligence can sometimes be alien to the human experience. In my case, I make people angry while minding my own business, and some people were upset over past lives I'm not so sure I believe in myself (let alone remember), so the advice fell a bit short. I practice radical nonjudgment with my clients, so while I can see why somebody else might attack them, I have no judgment as to whether it was deserved.

When a spiritual attack happens, most people wonder what they did wrong upon recognizing it. This is a normal, "I am appropriately aligned with society" question to ask. Because you are willing to ask this question, you are probably not the person who genuinely needs to soul-search over the root of a magickal attack. Unfortunately, the people who would most benefit from introspection—that group of people that do deserve a good cursing—are never going to ask themselves this question even if they wake up with pitchforks in their foreheads.

Realistically, people will find a variety of reasons to have a problem with you: for minding your own business, for having a different political outlook, or because you look weird in that color of shirt. Ultimately, you don't have to do anything but exist. Most of the time, the people who have these problems won't dig up a spellbook or work themselves into a lather and launch that energy at you. But a few do, and those who act out magickally do so often and to multiple people. It's often the same narrow subset of troublemakers acting on the general population. There may be complicated reasons that someone cursed or bespelled you rooted around power and control. These spells and their reasons may vary depending on your culture of origin, but it always comes down to either you having something someone wants or someone wanting you to do what they want you to do, regardless of your truth.

The reason why people attack doesn't matter for one simple reason: you can't control what other people do, nor can you control the way they see you. All you can do is protect yourself as best you can, respect boundaries and sacred space, and cultivate positive relationships with good, principled people while phasing out the toxic individuals as much as possible.

Assessing Damage

Before you visit a healer, spend some time assessing your damage. This introspection can give you and your healer clarity about what help you need. Use the following questions as journal prompts to assist you in that reflection.

The Debrief

- What happened?
- What do I know about the cause of what happened?
- What is my perspective on this incident? What is the perspective of the spirit or magick worker that directed this at me?

Emotions

- How do I feel about the experiences I just had?
- Am I questioning whether I experienced what I did? Am I rationalizing?
- Am I feeling aches and pains in my body as I think about how I feel? Where?
- What habits have I developed as a result of my recent experience? Do these habits serve me? Do these habits trigger emotions that inhibit the quality of my life?

Physical Health

- Did I sustain any physical injuries?
- How do I feel about those injuries?
- Am I feeling any pain, immobility, or discomfort that I did not before my experience began?
- Am I processing and interpreting sensation differently than I did before?

- How am I sleeping? Am I sleeping as normal for me? Are there any changes to my sleeping environment as a result of my experience?
- How is my immune system faring? Am I more prone to colds and illness than before?

Chakra Audit

Establish some space and time to yourself. Sit in a comfortable position and relax as much as you can. Starting at your root chakra and moving upward, focus on each chakra in turn. Spin it in multiple directions. Breathe through it from the front and then from the back of your body. If you have the mobility, explore yoga poses related to each chakra. Check to see if there's "stuff" in the chakra making it sluggish, and check for any holes.

If the chakras seem clogged, spend time breathing through them, using cool breaths and audible exhalation. Use the grounding exercises and energy hole methods described in chapter three to repair holes in your chakras. It may take several sessions to achieve a full repair. Help this process along by seeking out a Reiki healer or other appropriate person.

Household Recovery

After an attack/cursing, it's important to make sure you do a deep clean of your living space. If you struggle with limited energy for cleaning, just pick one surface a day to address. One day clear the table, the next wash the light fixtures, and so on. Treat it as if you are moving into a new home. Clear out old items you no longer need and get out all your cleaning tools, magickal and not. Move your furniture around, scrub floor to ceiling (one wall per day if that's all you can manage), and vacuum your carpets. If you can spring for carpet shampoo, do so. This deep clean removes all the old energy in your house. Once you have decluttered and cleaned to the best of your ability, start your magickal cleansing. If you want a total energy reset, clean with ammonia. Once finished, layer in the energies that you want. Burn protection incense at the windows, sprinkle a blessing or peace powder on the carpet or spray the walls with a potion made from whiskey.[7]

When cleansed to your satisfaction, seal off your work with a resin incense. Depending on your tradition, it might also be appropriate to make an offering to your ancestors.

Luck/Time/Circumstances

In Jason Miller's *Protection and Reversal Magic*, he mentions that a lingering effect of a cleared curse is sometimes the feeling of being out of phase with time.[8] I concur. While performing personal cleansings and uncrossing can help, getting back in sync with optimal reality may require petitioning fates or your patron spirits. The following ritual calls on you to tap into astrological symbols/the cosmos's powers to realign yourself with time and luck, as best fits your situation.

Ritual: Time Reset

This ritual should call out-of-time energies back to their correct places in the continuum. Crafted with astrological/planetary/time symbols, this ritual calls no deities. If you wish for a deity or spirit to partake in your working, you can always invite one.

---

7. You can find vacuum powders at botanicas and occult shops, or find a recipe to make your own online. Use sparingly, as these powders can clog even high-end vacuums.

8. Jason Miller, *Protection and Reversal Magick: A Witch's Defense Manual* (San Francisco: Red Wheel/Weiser, 2006), 188.

Depending on your practice, you can make an offering to any beings that spin the threads of Fate.

YOU WILL NEED:

Absolute quiet and space to yourself

A large floor space

An hourglass

A floor-sized conception of the zodiac wheel. Sometimes you can buy these, but you can also create your own with chalk, either directly on your floor or on a large tarp you use for this purpose

Marks on your ritual surface representing the four cardinal directions

Any altar to ancestors, deities, guiding spirits, and so on, especially those that take part in your regular practice

While I no longer believe that all ritual workings require containment, I believe *this* one does. In this situation, you need a circle or an equivalent energy construct because you are building an energetic clock. The clock represents the center of your being and your life story in this incarnation. This clock and astrological house chart is a snapshot of where you stand in the universe in all possible "right nows."

Set the hourglass in the center of the circle. From here, slowly ambulate the circle, moving forward with each step of the ritual after casting the circle and calling the quarters. If you are physically unable to walk around, you can make a smaller version of this chart and use your hands or a tool to circle it. You will move step by step until you come full circle.

CIRCLE CASTING:
At the center of the soul-star,
Where my heart connects to the universal pulse
I raise starlight—
From east to west
From south to north
Above and below.
And here, in this time without time
In this space without space
I invoke myself I invoke my Fate—
That all off-course shall reset,
That all move forward, for the best

FACING EAST:
I invoke the powers of air, the rulers of the stars of air:
Gemini, to restore my wit
Libra, to restore my balance
Aquarius, to restore my curiosity

FACING SOUTH:
I invoke the powers of the south, the rulers, and stars of fire:
Aries, to revivify my forces
Leo, to rebuild my confidence
Sagittarius, to allow me to move forward

FACING WEST:
I invoke the powers of water, the rulers of the stars of water:
Cancer, to restore my security
Scorpio, to repair my deepest mind
Pisces, to re-welcome magickal experiences

FACING NORTH:

I invoke the powers of earth, the rulers of the stars of the earth:
Taurus, to return all comforts taken
Virgo, to regain my sense of purity
Capricorn, to reanchor all that has meaning to me

Pick one of the twelve points on the floor and pick up the hourglass.

STAND IN THE ARC OF THE FIRST HOUSE: APPEARANCE/PRESENTATION/FIRST IMPRESSION

Stop at the first house. Say, "I ask the universe to correct all misalignment of the impression I make upon others." Flip the hourglass and wait for it to run out. When complete, move to the next house. You will repeat flipping the hourglass at each house.

STAND IN THE ARC OF THE SECOND HOUSE: MONEY

Stop at the second house. Say, "I ask the universe to correct all misalignment of the money I earn."

STAND IN THE ARC OF THE THIRD HOUSE: COMMUNICATION

Stop at the third house. Say, "I ask the universe to correct all misalignment of my communications in person or over other media."

STAND IN THE ARC OF THE FOURTH HOUSE: ANCESTORS

Stop at the fourth house. Say, "I ask the universe to correct all misalignment among my ancestors."

STAND IN THE ARC OF THE FIFTH HOUSE: PLEASURE

Stop at the fifth house. Say, "I ask the universe to correct all misalignment of that which brings pleasure to my life."

STAND IN THE ARC OF THE SIXTH
HOUSE: HEALTH AND WORK

Stop at the sixth house. Say, "I ask the universe to correct all misalignment of my health and employment."

STAND IN THE ARC OF THE SEVENTH HOUSE:
RELATIONSHIPS/PARTNERSHIP/MARRIAGE

Stop at the seventh house. Say, "I ask the universe to correct all misalignment of my partners and relationships."

STAND IN THE ARC OF THE
EIGHTH HOUSE: INHERITANCE

Stop at the eighth house. Say, "I ask the universe to correct all misalignment of what is rightfully mine."

STAND IN THE ARC OF THE NINTH HOUSE: FAITH

Stop at the ninth house. Say, "I ask the universe to correct all misalignment of my access to the energy stream of faith."

STAND IN THE ARC OF THE
TENTH HOUSE: REPUTATION

Stop at the tenth house. Say, "I ask the universe to correct all misalignment of my reputation and career."

STAND IN THE ARC OF THE ELEVENTH HOUSE: LUCK

Stop at the eleventh house. Say, "I ask the universe to correct all misalignment of my fortunes."

STAND IN THE ARC OF THE
TWELFTH HOUSE: UNCONSCIOUS

Stop at the twelfth house. Say, "I ask the universe to correct all misalignment of my deepest mind."

Once you complete the circuit for each house, set the hourglass at the center of the circle so that the sand falls, saying, "Let the courses move and then rest."

Bid goodbye to the elements and open the circle, stating, "May all that is right in this time and space be protected and remain so!"

Healing the Damage

In the case of a vampire attack, you may find that those injuries persist until you find an effective way to remove every cord. If you dealt with a situation that went on for over a week, find a person you trust to examine your aura. Regular healing work can often turn up things you thought you had removed because of the continuous digging through your energy layers. Sometimes repairing one psychic injury can cause previously ignored harm to rise to the surface. Because of this, stay as aware as possible not only of your psychic selves but of your mental health—so many psychic injuries are subconsciously self-inflicted, and sorting those out can be a lifelong project.

When Reiki Can't Help

For most people, visiting a Reiki healer after an attack does enough to fix the damage. But although Reiki is universal life energy, it is only one healing modality and healing energy type and cannot treat absolutely every spiritual injury that can happen. While the reasons for this remain unclear, some people are "allergic" to Reiki and may need a different modality. I have direct experience seeing Reiki do fantastic healing work for some people and damage a small but significant sample of others. Because this can happen, if you are a Reiki healer, please obtain verbal consent before healing someone. Also, pay attention to how a client is affected and listen when they report back their experience to you. Admit when something doesn't work.

Create a way of knowing when the Reiki or other energy work does and doesn't help. Often feedback from the person doing or receiving the healing should cover it. Sometimes, however, people have trouble communicating their real needs, so using different checks can help. You may need to use muscle testing, divination, or other methods of your own design. On the occasions that energy healing doesn't help, see if you can suss out why. There are practitioners advanced enough to place blocks on someone's ability to heal. Sometimes, because these attacks often link directly to personal traumas as a way of making the experience even worse, we subconsciously reject healing and adopt a curse into our senses of self. While overcoming shame is never as simple as saying "you have nothing to be ashamed of," it helps to start with internalizing that truth.

Medical Intervention
It's a good idea to get your health checked out by an allopathic doctor after long periods of being surrounded by negative energy. Stress changes our bodies. Other times our illnesses were already present—the negative experiences simply made us aware of them. Extended stress can exacerbate certain illnesses and cause others. Yes, visiting the doctor can be a fraught experience. You may have to choose between your mental health and your physical health due to what certain medical providers consider covered care. In the end, it's always better to know what's going on with your body because physical and mental health are deeply intertwined.

Theta Healing and Soul Retrieval

When I refer to the "soul," I speak of a roughly four-pound energy body that leaves our physical forms upon death. Although it takes considerable force for a practitioner to do so, some magickal workings can damage or fragment this body. Some of our metaphysical blips can result in—or be caused by—soul loss. Soul loss manifests in different ways depending on the person. One person may struggle to express love. Another may struggle to speak up when needed, and yet another may wind up trapped in anxiety at the most straightforward social situation. In the worst circumstances, people suffer from unshakable depression that resists all treatment. This depression is different from (but just as dangerous as) neurological depression. Most people in Western culture have some degree of soul loss, often due to unrecognized trauma. The single most effective way to correct soul loss is to see a skilled shaman about soul retrieval, engage in continuous introspection, and seek healing. Shamanic treatment is usually expensive, and it can be hard to find a legitimate, trustworthy practitioner. But getting such treatment also can have a lasting positive effect that reaches beyond healing magickal warfare and psychic attack.

In soul retrieval, the shaman goes on a trance journey and looks for the missing piece of someone else's soul. This piece can appear in different forms: a plant, animal, or mineral. Sometimes the shaman must battle for that piece and then do the work of placing it back in the right place within the person's energy fractals. The task is difficult and dangerous. Those who receive this treatment may feel as though they've regained parts of themselves thought lost forever. Some become connected to parts of themselves they never knew they had.

Soul Loss Assessment

If you want to dig deeper before seeking a shaman, you can also try the following meditation. Lie down in a safe place with a journal and pen nearby. Mentally trace the outline of your body, starting at your head and slowly moving to your feet. Look for a sense of connection—does it feel like any chunks are missing? Do any spots feel as though they don't belong to you or as if there's an absence of energy and flow? Those indicate spots where you need energy repair—and can, but do not always, indicate soul loss.

If you find a space where a chunk appears missing, focus on it. Make a note of any emotions or memories that arise when you focus on that space. Just receive what comes to you, reserving judgment. You may get flashes and images that make no immediate sense, especially in the form of colors, animals, plants, and nature scenes. When you finish this process, grab your journal and jot down everything you can recall. You may want to look up the symbolic meanings of the different visions you experienced. It can take a little time to understand the relevance of what you saw. This process does not let you reclaim a soul piece, but it gives you some ideas of where to look for ways to self-repair.

Protections, Immunities, and Inoculations

Many readers of this book also love urban fantasy and science fiction shows and thus are familiar with the "moral recap." After harrowing adventures, there's almost always a conclusion/exposition scene with one question summarizing the experiences: "What did we learn?" After periods of spiritual negativity, this question is especially important to ask. While these experiences are always terrible and sometimes even devastating, we learn from them ... or sometimes we unlearn. Through these experiences, we discover better ways to protect and prevent repeating negative experiences. Common lessons from my own experiences include learning the hard way that if you cut a deal with a spirit, follow through on your end of the bargain. Keeping toxic people in your life has long-term negative consequences. Removing the toxic people from your life often has short-term negative effects but long-term positive payoff. Every action has a consequence, *not* a judgment.

These experiences also invite you to look at your magickal practice. What did you find out you need to do better? What do you now know you're just plain bad at? What rules of magick apply to your situation that you had not previously considered?

Along with learning new ways to strengthen your wards, you also need to look at ways to establish immunities to certain types of spells. Sometimes you just need to protect yourself from radioactive spider bites (they never do give superpowers). It could involve establishing energetic blocking. Yes, the bind-outs mentioned in previous chapters can help; you may want to go so far as to create a mirror box so that even if you cross paths with that person, their energy just can't reach you.

Self-Care and Prevention

Practicing self-care may feel hard to do after the trauma of ongoing negativity. Because it might hurt, I encourage you to work on this in small chunks—but to keep showing up every day to work on the next section until it is complete. Take the question "What did we learn?" and make a nourishment map from the answers you discover.

Here you'll find a sample worksheet that can be included in any magickal records you keep, whether that's a Book of Shadows or a simple journal.

What Did We Learn?

- What protections do I use that are especially effective?
- What protection methods could use improvement?
- If something broke my house wards, how did they get in?
- If something invaded my energy, how did it enter? What self-doubts seemed most vocal at the time of entry?
- What can I add to my cleansing routines and practices to improve their effectiveness?
- Are there any ritual practices I need to quit for the time being?
- What are the limits of my usual go-to tools? How do I know a protective measure I am using isn't working?
- Do I know what led to this energetic situation?
- What did it teach me about human relationships?
- What did it teach me about boundary setting?
- How has this affected my sense of self?

Reinforcement Routines

When everything feels safe, we often set our security reinforcements aside. Then when we run into a conflict where someone might cast a curse, we end up scrambling to raise our defenses again. Possibly more annoying, when we have a regular protection practice, we may discover that someone has hacked it. This "hacking" is why it pays to remain proactive about changing methods of protection.

It's important to establish reinforcement routines and periodic changes in method. I encourage blending protection work into home routines, such as paying the bills and housework. So much of magickal work involves cleansing and clearing energy that it makes sense to try to save some steps through day-to-day integration. If you're already going to mop the floor, why not add some lemongrass tea to the bucket? If you're already scrubbing the toilet, you might as well add a little extra lemon juice to the bowl for clearing. If you're going to spend a few hours a day cleaning the kitchen, why not light a little protection incense? The ceremonially inclined may still enjoy more significant workings. Even so, such small, daily acts—coupled with periodically changing the spells, prayers, and substances used—can increase your overall metaphysical securities.

After everything has calmed down as though it never happened, acknowledge for yourself that what you experienced was real. Your feelings are real. Many things change the way we see the world, and psychic attack most definitely does. If you can find an open-minded therapist to talk to about your experience, do. If you can't get help right away, reach out anyway. Keep reaching out—someone out there will reach back.

TWELVE

FINAL NOTES FOR THE POTENTIALLY TRAUMATIZED

Whether it's curiosity or living hell that got you here, you've made it. There are other people out there struggling to get through a day without metaphysical crap flying at them. The slog to the next sunrise feels more severe than normal day-to-day troubles for these people sometimes to the point that they long for normal day-to-day struggles. If you're in such a place right now, here is what you can do: get up every day—even under that extra duress—and remind yourself: you got up. That's progress.

How and Why to Ditch Your Guilt

It's easy to stay in a bad situation because getting out requires behavior(s) under the label of "not nice." You pay the tax in setting boundaries by people objecting to you having them. You absolutely need them. Some people balk at reversal spells, hot foot spells, or other basic protections. In my opinion, this is the influence of toxic positivity, a worldview that only allows for what the person deems "positive" while ignoring all perceived negativity including anger, pain, and shame. When dark emotions go ignored, it does damage because trauma cannot be repaired without confronting some amount of spiritual negativity. Toxicity of this type all too often amounts to spiritual bypassing and victim blaming. Bad things happen no matter how positive your attitude, and attempting to fake positivity while in pain hurts more than just one person. People on the toxic positivity spectrum might raise moral objections, citing "harm none" as a reason to endure the torment. The refusal to fight back or cultivate spiritual allies to help end trouble comes from religious and social indoctrination. Because of this, I'm going to present a few ideas ranging from the heretical to the sacrilegious. You might need to embrace what you perceive as blasphemy to know peace.

First, church leaders can and do lie. Most of us grew up hearing that churches were havens of moral righteousness and absolute truth. Many houses of worship offer warm, nurturing, nonjudgmental communities. Sadly, entirely too many are very much the opposite.

Religious communities that bank on fear, shame, and silence to keep their memberships are far from moral. For many magickal practitioners, leaving such churches or other indoctrination forces presents us with the greatest inner battles of our lives. For those engaged in the occult, we often think we've broken with the rules and dogma instilled in us by these churches. We carry these indoctrinations with us and when life gets frightening, we often fall back on the unhelpful lessons we learned because they are familiar. Until we confront our real problems, we cannot reasonably defend ourselves from anything for an extended amount of time. We submit to poor treatment until we make an active effort to change the way we think.

There are also people outside toxic churches willing to violate the social contract of human decency. It is not up to you to hold these people accountable. Assume your spiritual burden is already adequate and has all it can hold, unless otherwise guided. It is, however, your duty to maintain healthy boundaries for yourself and your family. Sometimes you may need to use "not nice" magick to enforce those boundaries. What some people are taught as the "Christian thing" to do frequently perpetuates more abuse. This in no way speaks to the impressive capacity of some Christian magick workers.

Second, just as church leaders lie, other religious leaders can too. Leaders of other faiths can just as easily get an inflated view of their own moral superiority. All too often, it is the same dogma under a different label: "turning the other cheek" may be promoted as the so-called enlightened thing to do, but repetitive abuse no matter what the moral sales pitch does not enlighten anyone. Surrendering yourself to trauma delivered by others' hands doesn't make you more spiritual— it locks you in a negative cycle. Yes, I am talking about Pagan groups here too.

And finally, your anger does not make you a moral failure. Anger means that you *do* have a sense of moral boundaries; when treated properly, anger acts as an alarm system. Anger makes a wonderful ally because it can bring in a pool of energy to the work you do to enforce your boundaries. Even so, anger is tricky and can shift from friend to subvert enemy if not understood well. Be careful: anger likes to be the decision-maker, and it is bad at it.

When you find yourself struggling with guilt about what defensive magick might do to the receiver, ask yourself the following questions:

- Does your troublemaker care what happens to you? Are they holding back?
- If you do nothing, is this person going to stop, or just keep going until they feel they've won?
- How will your behavior change when you cut the negative energy or return it to its source?

Chances are, acting in self-defense will not change your character. Once you regain your peace, you might choose friends and interactions with more care. You will have increased self-knowledge. Beyond that, you will likely still have most of the same moral boundaries and make some new ones help you.

Mental Health Matters

When dealing with an abundance of energetic attacks, you're probably going to stigmatize yourself. In such a situation, many people talk about "feeling crazy," putting forth the possibility that they're "just imagining" the very real things happening to them. People around you might be oblivious to what you're sensing or tell you you're overly imaginative. Out of kindness, some are likely to point out emotional and spiritual issues you wrestle with all the time as probable causes of your distress. Your conditions may well inform you about the manner or type of attacks you're experiencing, so keep those in mind. If you already know what's normal for you, take stock of the *not* normal.

Do not minimize the impact of your experiences. Consider logical explanations. Seek mental health support wherever and whenever you can get it. Don't wait until it's all over to talk to someone. You may need to screen out therapists who see magickal thinking as a disease. That said, always get a full mental health screening—having a disorder does NOT invalidate your experience.

I repeat this often to my clients, and it bears repeating here: your mental health is your physical health. Emotional injury, the ability to concentrate and function, and the ability to feel safe are important. These can all affect your body. Treat your emotions and mentality with the same seriousness you do the rest of your body. Sometimes it happens that addressing mental health issues can ease physical discomforts.

Adversity Improves Witchcraft

As I write this, I do not doubt that I am the most competent witch I can be at this time in my life. Enemies, like lovers, are our teachers. I have had encounters with ones who were fierce, creative, and brilliant. I have also had encounters with the delicately narcissistic and milquetoast—now I can tell the difference.

When someone thrusts obstacles upon you, you either remove the obstacle or accept the limitation. Some people see the gain in limitation: it gives them an excuse. They don't have to try, and they shouldn't because look, they're cursed. Still, others do what they can and are just out of inner and outer resources. Others see these obstructions as the way they climb their personal Mount Everest. It's going to be rough getting there, but the reward upon arrival? Amazing.

The best thing you can do while you work to end these attacks is to find a way to benefit from them. I have learned to spirit trap, negotiate with beings I never imagined interacting with, and reframed my entire relationship with any religious concept whatsoever. I developed spells for what at the time seemed like the most impossible of challenges. I excavated deep talents within myself as well, talents I never had reason to seek.

No guide to counter-magick or protection can ever be exhaustive: so long as humans create, they will use that creativity for ends good and ill. And this is especially true because magick is a deeply creative and highly emotional art. Use this book as a place from which to work. Try things. Not everything will work. If something doesn't work, step back, use your divination methods, and think as creatively as you can. You will likely evolve new methods of defense unique to your life.

I wish you safety. I give you no moral admonishments. I bid you good mental health and encourage you to set your boundaries and to honor the boundaries of others. Remember: *no curse is unbreakable.*

RECOMMENDED READING

Like a lot of magickal folks, I do love my books. Sometimes reading up helps, and other times you end up in situations that no amount of reading or internet searching can resolve. What follows here are books I found helpful enough that I returned to them for inspiration and understanding as I constructed my spells, rituals, and defenses.

All of these books came in handy as a way to get me thinking differently. You may discover the same. Then again, I'm told by many people that I just don't approach anything like a normal person, whatever one of those is.

Keys to Perception: A Practical Guide to Psychic Development by Ivo Dominguez Jr.

Spirit Speak: Knowing and Understanding Spirit Guides, Ancestors, Ghosts, Angels, and the Divine by Ivo Dominguez Jr.

Psychic Attack by Draja Mickaharick

Spiritual Cleansing: A Handbook of Psychic Protection by Draja
Mickaharick

The Element Encyclopedia of 5000 Spells by Judika Illes

Magickal Formulary Spellbook I and II by Herman Slater

*Psychic Self Defense: The Definitive Manual for Protecting Yourself
Against Paranormal Attack* by Dione Fortune

*Hoodoo Herb and Root Magic: A Materia Magica of Afri-
can-American Conjure* by Catherine Yronwode

Protection and Reversal Magick: A Witch's Defense Manual by
Jason Miller

BIBLIOGRAPHY

Bromley, David. "Cults That Never Were: Satanic Ritual Abuse." Virginia Commonwealth University, 2009. Retrieved July 18, 2020. https://www.people.vcu.edu/~dbromley/undergraduate/spiritualCommunity/SatanicCults.html.

dagost27. "Eye Paint As a Protector and Medicine." In *Archaeology of Ancient Egypt 455*, edited by Ethan Watrall. East Lansing, MI: Michigan State University, 2012. Retrieved July 19, 2020. http://anthropology.msu.edu/anp455-fs12/2012/10/04/eye-paint-as-a-protector-and-medicine/.

"Demons and Demonology." Jewish Virtual Library. Retrieved July 18, 2020: https://www.jewishvirtuallibrary.org/demons-and-demonology.

Duvalier, James. "Performing a Spiritual Revocation." Retrieved July 18, 2020. http://jamesduvalier.com/spiritual-revocation/.

Gershman, Boris. "The Economic Origins of Evil Eye Belief." *Journal of Economic Behavior &*

Organization 110 (2015): 119–144. Retrieved June 4, 2020. https://ideas.repec.org/a/eee/jeborg/v110y2015icp119-144.html.

Hogeback, Jonathan. "Are Black and White Colors?" *Encyclopedia Britannica*, retrieved June 9, 2020. https://www.britannica.com/story/are-black-and-white-colors.

Humanities, Georgia. "Exhibition: Our Georgia, 1987–2007, Part One" Retrieved July 8, 2020. https://www.georgiahumanities.org/exhibition-our-georgia-1987-2007/.

Huson, Paul. *Mastering Witchcraft: A Practical Guide for Witches, Warlocks & Covens.* New York: Berkley Publishing Group, 1980.

"Italian Superstitions: The Evil Eye (Malocchio)." Ciao Pittsburgh. Retrieved July 4, 2020. https://www.ciaopittsburgh.com/italian-superstitions-the-evil-eye-malocchio/.

"Karma and Samsara." Vermont Hindu Temple. Retrieved July 15, 2020. https://www.vermonthindutemple.org/karma-and-samsara.

Marchini, Lucia. "Review—Spellbound." *Current Archeology,* October 19, 2018. Retrieved October 16, 2020. https://www.archaeology.co.uk/articles/review-spellbound.htm.

Miller, Jason. *Protection and Reversal Magick: A Witch's Defense Manual.* San Francisco: Red Wheel/Weiser, 2006.

Ogle, Marbury Bladen. "The House-Door in Greek and Roman Religion and Folklore." *The American Journal of Philology* 32, 3 (1911): 251–271. Retrieved June 8, 2020. https://www.jstor.org/stable/288616.

Onstott, Jane. *National Geographic Traveler: Mexico.* National Geographic, 2010. Retrieved June 8, 2020. https://books.google.com/books?id=Tgn2TZNbHy4C.

Owens, Christine Wilson. "Hmong." *Journal of Ethnomedicine,* June 1, 2007. Retrieved June 15, 2020. https://ethnomed.org/culture/hmong/.

Slater, Herman. *Magical Formulary Spellbook Book I.* New York: Magickal Childe, 1981.

"Smudging and the Four Sacred Medicines." Dancing to Eagle Spirit Society. Retrieved April 3, 2020. http://www.dancingtoeaglespiritsociety.org/medicines.php.

"Spiritual Work: When You Need to Control Someone." Hoodoo Roots. Retrieved June 20, 2020. http://www.hoodooroots.com/oldsite/control.htm.

Worth, Valerie. *The Crone's Book of Words.* Saint Paul, MN: Llewellyn, 1986.

INDEX

A

B

H

I

J

K

To Write to the Author

If you wish to contact the author or would like more information about this book, please write to the author in care of Llewellyn Worldwide Ltd. and we will forward your request. Both the author and publisher appreciate hearing from you and learning of your enjoyment of this book and how it has helped you. Llewellyn Worldwide Ltd. cannot guarantee that every letter written to the author can be answered, but all will be forwarded. Please write to:

Diana Rajchel
℅ Llewellyn Worldwide
2143 Wooddale Drive
Woodbury, MN 55125-2989

Please enclose a self-addressed stamped envelope for reply,
or $1.00 to cover costs. If outside the U.S.A., enclose
an international postal reply coupon.

Many of Llewellyn's authors have websites with additional information and resources. For more information, please visit our website at http://www.llewellyn.com

NOTES:

NOTES:

NOTES:

NOTES:

NOTES:

NOTES:

NOTES: